Remaking American Values

REMAKING AMERICAN VALUES

Challenge
to a Business Society

NEIL W. CHAMBERLAIN

Basic Books, Inc., Publishers

NEW YORK

The author gratefully acknowledges permission to reprint lines from "New Hampshire" from *The Poetry of Robert Frost* edited by Edward Connery Lathem. Copyright 1923, © 1969 by Holt, Rinehart and Winston. Copyright 1951 by Robert Frost. Reprinted by permission of Holt, Rinehart and Winston.

Library of Congress Cataloging in Publication Data

Chamberlain, Neil W
   Remaking American values.

   Includes index.
   1. Industry—Social aspects—United States.
2. Social values. 3. Business enterprises—United
States. I. Title.
HD60.5.U5C475   658.4'08   76-28754
ISBN: 0-465-06906-1

CONTENTS

Contents

IV
IN THE FACE OF CHALLENGE

PREFACE

SOCIAL VALUES and institutions are not so flexible that they readily adjust to accommodate new conditions—political, economic, and social. They do change, but they change slowly and reluctantly. For long stretches of time such laggard adjustment is usually sufficient to preserve both values and institutions. However, at some juncture the changes in conditions become just too formidable for slow accommodation. At that point if values and institutions are to serve their purposes swifter and more radical reform is needed. An upheaval in ways of thinking and acting is beyond the capacity of most incumbent leaders. They may be retired circumspectly and with honor, but a different leadership must take their place—a leadership with a new vision and fresh purpose, embracing values alien in important respects to those which have proved inadequate, a leadership which can restructure the major institutions in ways compatible with the new social vision.

Short of a military and bureaucratic dictatorship, such new values and revised institutional behavior cannot be imposed on an unwilling people. Rather, they must recommend themselves to the public because they promise to meet problems recognized as ineluctable, because they provide hope in the face of conditions which have eroded hope. No sudden moral conversion, no burst of light on the road to Damascus is called for. What is needed is only the relentless wearing down of general belief in the old political faith, the old economic creed, what its most devout followers nostalgically refer to as ''the old time religion.'' When one faith has been lost, a new one will sooner or later take its place.

The present social order in the United States largely derives from its business leadership, whose composition and outlook have changed over the years, adapting to the political, geographical, technological, economic, and social changes which have confronted it. Its leaders, modest about their power, generally disclaim any direct influence on the social values which have evolved in America. In the same breath however, they argue a mutual reinforcement, if not identity, between America's values and their business institutions, a linking of their own survival and the survival of traditional values. This latter position is the more realistic one.

It is no adverse reflection on the past accomplishments of the business sector to suggest that the United States is now moving into a period when a conjuncture of political, economic, and social circumstances is inexorably forcing a pace and direction of change with which many of our present business leaders simply are unable to cope. Geared to a pattern of minimal modification in their established practices and ways of thinking—concession for survival— they are incapable of the larger leaps which changing conditions are calling for, ever more insistently.

Nevertheless, it is out of this business class that I expect the new leadership to emerge, not suddenly or apocalyptically but at a pace and with a vigor that overwhelms the old practitioners. The running of our technologically and economically complex society calls for individuals who have been trained to think imaginatively and realistically not only about political power but about economic organization. They are most likely to be found among a small but expanding number of young people who are at the same time fascinated and repelled by business, who delight in political problem-setting and managerial problem-solving, but who cannot with equanimity face a lifetime of pursuing business goals which strike them as increasingly remote from the major problems of our times. This growing number of young men and women will willingly abandon the present corporate mold and its associated social values, which they regard as outworn and ineffective.

While working within established businesses they will not hesitate to advance a new, more socially oriented business ideology. They will function as advocates for a cause, both within the business world itself and among public policy makers. Reform, when it comes, must be initiated outside of business, but it will be effective only if it makes sense to enough business leaders to make the new system work. To give it that appeal, it is necessary for business to participate in the design. That participation, I anticipate, will come—enthusiastically, not reluctantly—from a small, respected, and dynamic group which has a different vision of the place of business in contemporary society. The members of this group will work to put in place a new pattern of business activity, experimenting as they go, their efforts reinforced by the pressures of the challenging world.

It is changes in the corporate structure which hold the key to changes in social values—one cannot come without the other. New corporate forms more calibrated to the needs of our times are possible, embodying values which are appropriate to those needs while still preserving the best of the past. I have tried to suggest some of the possibilities, without in any sense attempting to draft a blueprint.

This is a continuation of a process of thought which I began in a book entitled, somewhat misleadingly, *The Place of Business in America's Future: A Study in Social Values,* and carried on in *The Limits of Corporate Responsibility.* In the first, I developed at some length the concept of social values which is the springboard for the present work. The second explained in detail why I had concluded that large-scale corporate enterprise would be unable to ameliorate greatly some of the major problems for which society has come to hold it responsible.

I have many, many intellectual debts, only some of which I have been able to recognize. Others, I am afraid, I may have once been able to identify but have now forgotten. There are some debts, I am sure, of which I have been unconscious even in the past, ideas seeded but lying dormant for a time. I have more immediate debts of gratitude to Barbara Sorich and Carol Gillis, and especially to Wilda Hayes, for their responsive and capable secretarial assistance, and to the Faculty Research Fund of the Graduate School of Business, Columbia University, for its financial assistance.

I

THE ISSUE
OF VALUES

1

The Best Is Past, or the Failure of Values

WHEN the often-cited nineteenth-century French historian, Alexis de Tocqueville, visited and surveyed the young American republic in the 1830s, he was struck by—among other things—the optimism and ebullience which he encountered. The great majority of the nation "have all a lively faith in the perfectibility of man . . . ; they all consider society as a body in a state of improvement, humanity as a changing scene, in which nothing is, or ought to be, permanent; and they admit that what appears to them today to be good, may be superseded by something better tomorrow." [1]

That same sense of aggressive optimism continued to characterize expanding America throughout the rest of the century. Largely free of class constraints and of inherited poverty, the country had seemingly boundless opportunities. Still largely land-oriented, it looked to a larger future ("alabaster cities . . . , undimmed by human tears") and believed in its destiny ("manifest"). It regarded with extravagant pride its self-devised government ("with liberty and justice for all''). Apostrophized by Tocqueville as ''a democracy more perfect than antiquity had dreamed of,'' America viewed itself as the pattern on which the rest of the world should and ultimately would be molded.

Despite the scourge of civil war, the occasional stumbling of the economy, and a few bloody labor strikes, which raised the specter of class division, America continued on its self-congratulatory way into the twentieth century. As late as the eve of the Great Depression, Robert Frost could lament that American authors lacked tragic stimulus. ''It makes the guild of novel writers sick/to be expected to be Dostoievskis/on nothing worse than too much luck and comfort.''

The contrast of that ebullient spirit with today's pessimism and despair is too evident to require comment. ''We are no longer confident about our uniqueness and superiority. . . . Our dreams of endless progress and economic omnipotence have dissolved. . . . [Our] problems [are] more obdurate than expected, more likely to worsen under prescription.'' [2] The file of writers who have played on these themes over the last few years continues to lengthen. Intellectuals of as widely differing perspectives as Herbert Marcuse, Andrew Hacker, Richard Goodwin, and Robert Heilbroner have arrived at very nearly the same dead end. We have become accustomed to books with such titles as *The End of the American Era, The Chaotic Society,* and *The Age of Anxiety.*

The principal cause of the pervasive pessimism seems to be a belief that our values have failed us. Somewhere there was a wrong turning; somewhere American society went astray and arrived at a dead end. The inadequacy of our values is perceived in a variety of ways. There are some who believe that our old and honored values have been mindlessly trivialized and perverted and that the faith of our fathers should be recovered and restored. They feel that the permissiveness of the present age undermines probity and self-discipline; parental indulgence and public provision sap self-reliance. Others are convinced that some of America's most ingrained values, such as material satisfaction and individualism, have been carried too far and are wrong for the future. New values must be developed—but what, and how? Still others are convinced that our social values *will* change—the times demand it—but they will change in a direction that can only be viewed as undesirable, as, for example, toward readier acceptance of political authority, even totalitarianism.

I share the conviction that social values are at the root of our trials today. The values we now have are not serving us well; they are both creating some of our difficulties and preventing us from solving others. But that is to start the story in the middle. Before we can say where our values are deficient and what then can be done about them, it is first necessary to identify what they are, how they came to exist, and how they have changed. Without such an exploration any platform lacks foundations. Without some definition of social values enabling us to trace their origins and development, any analysis is reduced to the level of a Sunday editorial.

For example, if our values have led us to a dead end, we are entitled to know why there was no prior change in direction before the dead end was reached. Is our society composed of children following some Pied Piper? If we are exhorted to adopt new social values more suited to the needs of the day, what reason is there for expecting consensus in the face of social fragmentation?

The thesis which pervades the present examination is the centrality of business to social values in the United States. It is the major business institutions that have been the carriers of American values—values which they have fostered and under which they have thrived. But these same values too have become enmeshed with the American identity. They are an essential ingredient in the way Americans think about themselves. They have become a part of the national character. This is not some shabby trick or sinister conspiracy which business interests have put over on the people. On the contrary, business has been the leading edge of a way of life which Americans have found congenial.

In order to understand how business fell into its role as the carrier wave of social values, two types of analysis are needed. The first is a theoretical formulation, a paradigm, in present parlance, of how social values are formed and how they change. The second is an historical examination of value formation in the United States.

The roots of contemporary values lie in business soil; one cannot be spaded without turning over the other. To appreciate how our values inhibit business change, and how business inhibits value change, the relationship between the two must be established. Only then can we appreciate how contemporary challenges to our values constitute challenges to business as we know it, and why any reconstruction of values depends on a reconstruction of the business corporation.

The story begins with an introduction of the leading characters, the social values themselves.[3] They are three in number, emerging as answers to the three philosophical questions with which every society must come to grips: 1) what constitutes "the good life"? 2) what is the proper exercise of coercive authority in creating and maintaining the social order? 3) how are the benefits of society to be distributed?

Most societies harbor within themselves not just one conception but an array of beliefs or theories as to what constitutes the good life. Some beliefs perhaps are asserted by a handful of individuals and some, perhaps, by a sect or profession or ethnic group. When one conception from among this array eventually wins a wider following than the others, and is assimilated by more and more individuals in the course of their maturation, it becomes modal. In fact, it eventually becomes the commonly accepted standard by which any person's achievements can be judged successful or not and answers the question of what a society values most. This we shall call the *focal value*. Over the ages, the focal values which have been repeated most often have been some variant of a religious, militaristic, or materialistic orientation.

This does not mean that once a particular theory of what constitutes the good life has become the dominant expression of a society it eliminates all others. They are simply subordinated. Nor need the focal value be displayed with elemental purity. As the adopted expression of various differentiated individuals and groups, it often assimilates into one compatible whole components which are only im-

6

perfectly related. An overriding drive for material satisfaction may be accompanied by religious conviction. In the United States, for example, the widely advertised Protestant ethic has supported the competitive striving for private wealth without offending Catholic minorities, even though occasionally threatening them with a prejudice used for competitive advantage.

Nor need a focal value be monistic. In some rare instances a society has sought a many-sided life—a due regard for material satisfaction, a sense of religious identity, the elation of response to physical challenge (as in personal sports and combat), and aesthetic appreciation, all held in some consciously sensed balance. Balance itself becomes focal. This conception seems to have characterized, for example, Periclean Athens and Cosimo Medici's Florence. Unfortunately, in most societies too few people have the capacity to express themselves nobly in a number of ways for a focal value of balance to win a wide following. More often, stress is placed on some singular value which is within the capacity of a larger proportion of the population. It is not surprising that the focal value which has swept the modern world is materialistic accumulation, or, more generally, consumption, which requires no special talents.

The second value question which a society must confront involves the use of coercive force in social relationships—who should exercise it, in what forms, over whom, and to what ends. As in the case of the focal value there is a spectrum of opinion within a society as to the degree of conformity which can ethically be coerced. One end of the spectrum emphasizes social coherence, order, and reliance on hierarchic authority; the other pole stresses individual discretion and personal autonomy. When some consensus emerges as to the proper or acceptable use of coercion in maintaining a desirable order, we shall call this the *constitutional value*.

The United States has been frequently chided for the informal coercion which popular opinion exercises over dissidents—the tyranny of the majority, "mobocracy." It has been even more frequently lauded and its people envied for their freedom from state control. But however gloved the hand of coercion, or whatever its terminological label, some authority necessarily controls the individual whenever social policy is made or social relationships enforced. The more orderliness that is sought (freedom from chance, from the unexpected, from the unpleasant), the less room there is for individual idiosyncrasy. The more urgently social objectives are pursued, the less opportunity there is for personal discretion.

The third social value relates to the distribution of rewards. Unless a society is willing to leave the question of how it allocates the benefits it creates purely to the play of power, in a Hobbesian war of each against every other, it requires some ethical justification for the distribution of wealth and status. To be generally accepted it must satisfy people's sense of justice. By what principle should some benefit more than others? Why should there not be a more equal division? How equal should it be? If those with superior advantages choose not to justify their condition solely on the ground that they have somehow obtained "title" to it, under a system which has conferred or recognized (has in fact *made*) that title, they are driven to derive some principle which justifies their disproportionate share, both to themselves and to those with less.

Three distinct principles of distribution have been emphasized in one society or another, at one time or another, both singly and sometimes in combination. These are the principle of inheritance (of wealth, social position, and perquisites), the principle of competitive achievement, and the principle of egalitarianism. Since a society has different kinds of advantages to distribute, it may sanction one principle for one kind of advantage and a different one for another kind of advantage (the egalitarian principle for access to education, for example, but inherited position for access to property rights). Usually one of the three principles assumes overriding importance, however, and colors a society's outlook on distributive matters generally. We shall call this the *distributive value*.

These social values—focal, constitutional, and distributive—collectively help to establish a society's identity, giving it coherence and continuity. The three values are interrelated in subtle and complex ways. Rational materialism may be linked with a belief in constitutional individualism which requires distributive inequalities, or it may be tied to an egalitarian philosophy which can be achieved only by a centralized authority. Focal religious values may be coupled with Catholic centralism or Lutheran autonomy, and associated with sumptuary privileges of office or the purest form of communal living. Whatever the interrelationships of the three value strands, they weave together to create bonds of community, a shared perspective of social life, linkages between the constituent parts—until or unless circumstances begin an unraveling process which saps the unifying strength of the value core.

We shall be concerned in this study with identifying the value strands which have jointly made the American identity, both self-perceived and as perceived by others, and seeing how those values have changed over time. But before beginning that historical, empirical investigation, let us pursue a little further the theoretical question of how specific values get selected from the array of possible choices—the process by which some focal value becomes modal, some constitutional value wins general acceptance, and some consensus emerges as to the distributive value.

2

How Social Values
Are Formed

A COMPLEX SOCIETY such as that of the United States
spawns a number of diverse groups. Some, such as ethnic and racial
groups, are consanguineous; some, such as religious and political
bodies, are consensual. Still others, among them professional, vocational, or recreational associations, are functional. Groups divide
and merge, become more amorphous or more specialized, grow or
decline in number of members, acquire special influence, or are
ignored.

Each such group, itself a small society, has its own focal, constitutional, and distributive values. These give it its own special sense of
identity, distinguishing it from the numerous other groups with
which it interacts. Its values serve as a means of reinforcing the solidarity of the group, advancing its special interests, and of excluding
those whose interests differ.

Some groups, for example, a college alumni association, or a literary society, are so limited in their objectives that they have little impact on others. Conversely, other groups, such as a national political
party or a labor federation, have an actual or potential influence on
the whole of a society.

How Social Values Are Formed

At any period in a society's history, circumstances and conditions conjoin in such a way that they favor the rise of some one group to a position of special strength and importance. For whatever reason—social upheaval, economic development, geographical expansion, international conflict—that group seems especially equipped to deal with the conditions the society confronts, to provide leadership or set an example for the rest of society. It emerges as the major influence; wins support from those who will benefit by its advance; effects alliance with other strategic groups; elicits the tolerance of still others (especially those to whom success itself is magnetic); and is observed noncommittally in its upward climb by the often larger numbers of less concerned or uninvolved members of the population.

The group which thus rises to a special position succeeds over time in impressing on the society the particular set of values which characterizes it. It need not employ force in achieving this end; it simply makes manifest, through its widening influence, the growing identity between its own and the nation's welfare. It is the *acceptance* of the group's social role by others, for whatever reasons and however long it takes that acceptance to ripen, that gives special status to its values.

The values of other groups within the society are not extirpated but submerged. The assortment of group values may be as diverse as before the rise of the dominant group, but the hold of these particularistic values on their members is muted and compromised. In the United States, for example, religious associations and educational institutions retain their separate identities and creeds. However, these are compatible with the dominant business-oriented values, and the religious associations and educational institutions adapt themselves to those values, reinforcing them. Labor unions at first opposed the values associated with corporate enterprise, but the American Federation of Labor dates its origins from its decision to accept the business system, asking only that business accept it.

In the process of shaping the national identity in this fashion, the dominant group modifies its own values. As it associates its interests with the interests of all society, it develops a wider orientation which blurs somewhat its previous particularistic concern. A religious authority makes room for the coercive use of military power and the secular demands of trade. A business leadership makes concessions to the spirit of solidarity and fraternity characterizing labor groups. Nevertheless, the group's own interests continue to be paramount. Why· else should any group strive to extend its influence? The justification for such preferential treatment is easy to come by. Since the national welfare has become more closely identified with the values of a particular group, that group must remain dominant in order to advance the national welfare. The justification, however circular, is sufficient. It is sufficient, that is, if enough people have been convinced that the coercive sanctions which are applied to maintain the social order are ethically justified because they serve larger interests than those of a favored few. The dominants acquire their advantages only if they have managed to link their own values and interests to those of society at large.

To describe a group as dominant is not to imply that it can have its own way. It suggests only that if it is strong enough to impress its values on the society it can advance its own interests to a greater extent than other groups. Nevertheless, it must often make concessions to other groups which are important to its success or survival. These concessions are not always formally negotiated or legislatively documented, though formal negotiation and legislation may take place. The "terms" of relations between groups are inferred from challenges and responses in a number of situations, so that each group learns how far it can go before inviting retaliation, and what the nature of retaliatory sanctions is likely to be. For example, in England, throughout the nineteenth century, the rising bourgeoisie confronted the dominant but declining landed aristocracy, the two groups testing their relative strengths in repeated political encounters, occasionally redefining in parliamentary terms the state of their joint accommodation.

Because the network of accommodations, which is always in process of being confirmed or revised, is so indirectly arrived at, we can refer to it as an implicit bargain. The strength or weakness of the dominants, the extent to which their values have achieved primacy within the society, is reflected in the terms of the implicit bargain which is continuously being negotiated with the other groups whose influence, while secondary, still counts.

This continuous negotiation, while necessarily involving the dominant group, does not always or even usually involve it directly. Since the spread of representative government in the nineteenth century, a class of professional politicians has sprung up to solicit office from the electorate. Elected officials, unlike the dominants, do not acquire the power to impress their values on society, unless they abandon the representative role and seek to impose themselves on society by conspiracy, force, or demagoguery. Otherwise, professional politicians serve only a limited term of office, are subject to replacement by other politicians even of a different party, and, most importantly, are able to exercise leadership only by working within the existing system of power relationships. Politicians, in effect, become brokers of power, ascertaining where major influence lies and seeking to accommodate or harness it. They assist in defining the terms of the implicit bargain.

Even in those instances when a politician or reform party succeeds in putting together a coalition of subordinate interests which is voted into office despite dominant opposition, the politician or party faces the ineluctable necessity of making the social-economic-political system work, and the "little" interests, however much in revolt, can seldom oblige with such a performance. They usually lack the necessary administrative skills, the substantive knowledge, and the network of associations to run society's major institutions. They can perhaps impede their effective functioning, by strike, sabotage, demonstrations, or violence, but they are less capable of making them run again, or at least making them run effectively. The contemporary world has yet to see a capitalist society voted out and a socialist society voted in, successfully, by democratic political process. Even Marxist opinion has been vacillating on the feasibility of such a peaceful revolution. The abortive administration of the late President Salvador Allende in Chile is illustrative of the difficulty. It is irrelevant that Allende was hampered by international opposition, since that opposition itself reflected interests allied with Chile's deposed dominants.

Professional politicians may of course use their office to modify the existing balance of power. They may, for example, facilitate the enactment of legislative protection of labor's right to organize, so that workers become too solidly unionized to be repressed as easily as formerly. The balance of power between business interests and organized labor will then necessarily undergo change, as it did in the United States following the New Deal administrations of Franklin D. Roosevelt. But this only means a modification of the implicit bargain, not its replacement.

Thus over the years professional politicians move into and out of office, while the dominant group within the society continues to determine, more than any other group, the framework within which those politicians perform. Moreover, the conservatism which this implies is abetted by other governmental arms, in particular the bureaucracy and the judiciary. The bureaucracy administers, the judiciary interprets and enforces *existing* law. The first is generally long-tenured, the second sometimes so, notably in the U.S. Supreme Court. Both serve as a protective shield to the dominants, commonly striking down the attempted changes in practices which a dissident group may be seeking for its own advance. Like the dominants themselves, once they have achieved their position, both bureaucracy and judiciary prefer to be guided by precedent. As long as the effects of changes in external conditions can be forestalled, the old routines continue, on the side of prevailing order.

Despite this inherent conservatism, popular representative government does make a difference in the security and strength of a dominant group. By encouraging expressions of public dissatisfaction, democratic political forms make it necessary for politicians to appeal to popular sentiment to win or keep office. Dominant interests are obliged to make concessions, to give some semblance of responsiveness to popular demands. Even if the concessions are modest, and even if the effect of the legislation in which they are embedded is eroded with the passage of time, representative government has a cumulative restraining effect on any dominant class. At the very least it exacts a greater effort to defend position and privileges.

A society's values—its conception of what constitutes the good life, its sanctioned use of coercive authority, its sense of equity in the distribution of benefits—can hardly be cherished and endowed with emotional content if they are viewed simply as part of the success story of a particular interest group, somewhat watered down by the implicit bargains effected through the brokerage function of professional politicians. If a society's values are to maintain a hold on people's minds and secure the dominants in their position, they must be given a philosophical validation. The writings of intellectuals, both past and present, are drawn on to clothe a society's values in more durable, more effective, more disinterested language. Gradually there builds up a body of literature and doctrine which becomes the venerated expression of a society's beliefs, lending itself to exegesis and elaboration with the passage of time, to which additions can and continue to be made.

John Locke is particularly important to the philosophical validation of America's values. From his *Two Treatises on Government* derive many of the great statements on individual liberty, the rights of property, and the limited role of government. The Declaration of Independence, the Federalist papers, the opinions of certain literate jurists like Oliver Wendell Holmes, Jr., the essays of Ralph Waldo Emerson, the poetry of Walt Whitman, and the fiction of Mark Twain (or at least portions of them) are other examples of how America's social values have been given a more enduring philosophical and emotional content. If practice deviates from profession, the deviance is lamented, distinguished, or ignored, but the piety is preserved.

Even when there are shifts in the social balance of power, so that the implicit bargain must be modified, the philosophical validation is not replaced by some new, more relevant doctrine. It is too much the shape and shaper of a society's identity to change like a suit of clothes. Instead, it is reinterpreted, as the Supreme Court reinterprets the Constitution to meet changing social needs, and is supplemented by fresh inspiration.

We shall shortly explore in greater depth how the business class rose to dominance in the United States, affirming values which won such widespread approval that they became identified with American society. But first one more piece must be fitted into the theoretical structure. Obviously social values are not rigid or they could not last. They are modified in the passage of time, not in any biological sense but in terms of event-filled history. What is subject to modification, however, is also subject to more radical change. We are interested in the process by which both modification and such change occur.

3

How Social Values
Are Changed

SOCIAL VALUES, once seeded, have a protracted existence. The dominant classes which sowed them have usually remained dominant long enough to perpetuate a set of values for extended periods, even centuries, despite modifications which have been necessary to accommodate changing conditions. Such alterations do not threaten value continuity as much as they assure it. The American constitutional value of individualism retains a strong popular appeal despite the obvious difficulty in applying a frontier concept to highly organized corporate society. As long as it is reinterpreted in ways satisfying most people under the changed conditions, it survives to preserve the more important principle of freedom of enterprise.

Occupying positions of strategic power, a dominant class has available to it techniques of self-protection not given to other groups, or at least not given in as full a measure. In the face of prolonged opposition from an intransigent group, it can undermine that group by co-opting its leaders or by making concessions to its members. The American labor movement, for example, is on the whole a willing supporter of private business institutions, from which its constituent unions have bargained substantial benefits. Few individuals would feel more threatened by political radicalism than our present labor officials. It would cast them adrift on an unknown sea, with no destination of their own and with no independent seamanship if they had a destination. In any challenge to corporate power, business leaders—barring any egregious mistakes of their own—can count on union support, even though unions are ready enough to chip away at specific business practices to shift the implicit bargain in their favor.

If, despite concession and co-optation, opposition to a dominant group continues, repression by force is possible, since a dominant class understandably has close links with the forces maintaining order. This is not a matter of callous exercise of brutality motivated by self interest, but a philosophically rationalized though unfortunate intervention to preserve a way of life which is identified with society's welfare.

Nevertheless, there are limits to the effectiveness of these means of maintaining the existing social values. Perhaps no theme has been so often expressed as the impermanence of power and the decline of dominance, both of nations and of groups or classes within nations. It is only a conjunction of circumstances which leads to a particular group's impressing its values on a society at some point in time. But circumstances change, and the conjunction of events which was once so auspicious begins to unravel. New forces intervene, with which the once-favored group is less able or less willing to cope. Its dominant position begins to be eroded.

The circumstances and objective conditions which are subject to change are numerous and potent. They include such broad categories as economic and technological conditions, international political relations, and the condition of the population itself, such as its size, age, and ethnic composition, its rate of growth, and its level of education.

These objective conditions undergo change at uncertain rates and in uncertain directions, sometimes slowly and incrementally by social evolution, sometimes precipitously and unpredictably by intrusive events. The changes may create what some subordinate group within a society perceives as new opportunities for its own advancement. This group experiments, risks breaks with tradition, and becomes more energetic in taking advantage of the new circumstances. We shall call such a group a thruster. Its efforts may be sharply focused in a revolutionary surge to make good, but they may also be gradually cumulative, almost self-revelatory, so that any newly achieved position comes almost as a surprise, requiring time to become accustomed to.

Thus it was that the objective conditions of increasing population, the ambitions of competing nation-states, the spread of empires, an increasing secularization of thought, and a growing interest in science all conjoined in the late eighteenth and early nineteenth centuries to provide opportunities for a class of entrepreneurial opportunists, allowing them, who otherwise would have been dependent on a landed aristocracy, to establish new positions of influence for themselves. Scorned by that aristocracy and by the professional classes, these businessmen and industrialists—the bourgeoisie—began as thrusters and ended as dominants.

Thrusters are likely to have a stronger sense of personal or group objectives and to exhibit more ambivalence towards the existing values and codes of society. They are likely to be less satisfied with their status, hence more receptive to changes in the established order. Of course, some may only be seeking greater recognition within the existing society, looking for a greater degree of acceptance without shaking the system. Of course, a thruster group may fail because it is uncertain of its own intentions or because it is shunted aside by another more purposeful thruster group. And naturally, there is no guarantee that a thruster group, however purposeful, will unseat the dominant class, over however long a period of time.

Nevertheless, if objective conditions indeed have changed in ways which the dominants have difficulty in accommodating themselves to, and if the thrust is vigorous and sustained, whatever measure of success the challengers achieve is likely to draw to them their own supporters and allies, their own coterie of those who admire success, and other groups of lesser or more timid thrusters who see their own futures benefited by a shift in loyalty.

The old dominants may seek to counter, and a contest may ensue, often over an extended period of time and with an uncertain outcome. But the position of the old dominants, based on conditions which no longer obtain, is bound to become more tenuous. Conversely, the power of an authentic rising thruster class, riding on a new conjuncture of forces, spreads within the society.

But no power is certain, especially the power of a group which has to learn a new role. If the thrusters aspire to slip into the seat of primary influence, they necessarily must inherit responsibility for the successful functioning of the social-political-economic system. There is no escaping coming to terms with those on whose cooperation they in part depend or accommodating others whose goodwill or at least tolerance is essential. The rising dominants in an effort to placate the declining dominants, may be willing to muddy or obscure their own position to avoid too direct a confrontation of values. Old values lag on and are not easily dislodged from the minds of people. Some aspects of the traditional values may not be particularly important or vexatious to the new dominants, so that they are content to leave them in place. The former elite may be allowed to retain status and custom, the new dominants deferring in some respects, perhaps gaining some advantage from the continuity with past glory, perhaps even relishing a bit the color of behavioral patterns which have no impact on the main drift. Thus the English bourgeoisie for many generations, even while asserting more and more vigorously a new social vision, did little to dislodge the landed aristocracy from its positions of social privilege, as long as it did not seriously block the path of change.

Despite any such conciliatory efforts, the most significant aspects of the conversion of thrusters into dominants is that as their expanding role becomes accepted, reflecting the shift in national temper, the values which they carry will emerge, inevitably if gradually, as the new social values. As the new leaders, in time, influence or control the decision positions of the major institutions, their way of life and modes of thinking gradually spread out and infect one after another component group in the society.

This result emerges almost imperceptibly. As the thrusters acquire greater influence in the social order, they use that influence to establish the standards by which antagonistic individuals and groups are screened out from the centers of social decision and others, more congenial and supportive, are allowed in. Within other (non-thrusting) groups, those individuals who can most effectively work with the thrusters-become-dominants rise to the leadership positions. The former leaders have been too closely identified with the old dominants to change their attitudes and allegiances; for the good of the organization, they must be replaced with fresh blood that can establish an easier rapport with the new centers of influence. As a consequence, and without any heavy-handed intervention by the new dominants, other groups tend to become oriented toward them. In the decades following the American Civil War, for example, the churches, universities, government agencies, the military, ethnic groups, voluntaristic, and eleemosynary organizations, professional associations and even labor unions all increasingly tended to choose leaders who could effectively work with the increasingly more entrenched business class.

There can be thrusters and dominants in every group, no less than in society as a whole. This is also true of the dominant group; all of its members do not see alike, do not possess identical views on values, or react in precisely the same ways to changing objective conditions. This means—the point should be emphasized—that a challenge to the dominant leadership of a society may come not only from outside thrusters, but also from thruster elements within the dominant group itself. A Luther challenged the established church not with intent to displace the institution, but to alter its values so radically, from within, as to displace its incumbent hierarchy. The difference is the difference between rebellion and revolution, but in both cases the effect is a transformation of values.

For purposes of clarity let us reserve the term "thruster" only for those factions or groups which contend with the dominants of society as a whole, for our purposes not applying it to factions seeking change within lesser groups. Thus an *inside* thruster group is possible *only* within a dominant class. To avoid any confusion, we shall use the term "thruster" only for those groups which are the carriers of a different set of values from the incumbent dominants. Thus when we speak of inside thrusters we are not referring to a perhaps disgruntled younger generation of a dominant class, impatient to take over the reins and display a different leadership *style*. We mean a group, young or old, within the dominant class, which is so dissatisfied with both the role of its class and its own role within that class that it attempts to displace the established leadership and to reorient the dominant institution to ends different from those it presently serves.

To foreshadow the outcome of our inquiry, the thesis will be advanced that changes have indeed occurred in American society which seriously weaken the position of its most influential group, its business leadership. That group continues to function with values which are less and less appropriate to the changed conditions, and with a belief that good-faith concessions and stepped-up co-optation will suffice to maintain the values which it prizes and to which a large number—most probably a majority—of the American people still subscribe. But if objective circumstances have indeed changed, a reluctance to give up traditions (and advantages) is simply irrelevant to the outcome, and even a present broad base of support can evaporate in the face of impotence to cope with those changes.

These changed conditions can only be met through the assertion of a new and more appropriate set of values, from a thruster group elbowing aside the incumbent dried-up leadership that is barnacled with outworn values. That thruster group must be able to make society work. Given the institutional complexity and the inescapable importance of the economic sector (under any set of values), the greatest likelihood is that it will come from within business itself—an inside thruster group.

That is the outcome of our inquiry. To reach it we will use the abstract formulation of value formation and change set out in this and the preceding chapter, applying it to the United States. We will first inquire how business came to play its dominant role in American society and explore in what ways its influence has shaped the values American society professes. Then we will analyze the challenges which are being offered to our present values and whether there is any basis for believing that the challenges can be met while still preserving those values. If not, and if changes in values are called for, then, finally, we will look for signs of possible thruster groups on the American scene, with a potential for directing American society in ways more suited to changed conditions.

When conditions do change, we confront them as facts. We cannot avoid them simply because we do not like them. But if we—or a thruster, with our support—can also confront them as opportunities we may be able to create a different and preferable way of life. Pessimism may be out of place.

4

Thrusters and Dominants
in American Society

IN THE CENTURY and a half prior to the American Revolution, colonial society had produced its own upper class—some even said an aristocracy. Although the undeveloped state of the economy allowed few to enjoy leisure while others toiled, some men toiled alongside those who toiled for them too. The ranks of yeomen and artisans had gradually accommodated a landed gentry ("planters," as Benjamin Franklin referred to them) and mercantile families, so that colonial societies became graded by wealth and class. Alan Simpson remarks that the Rhode Island commonwealth founded by Roger Williams, the "Irrepressible Democrat," offered "no resistance to the emergence of a little colonial aristocracy built out of fortunes in land and trade and concentrating effective power in its own hands," [1] and the same could be said of the other colonies.

Comprised of men of affairs and enlightened citizens, this native aristocracy was usually closely associated with the local representatives of the English government. Although this charmed circle perpetuated itself, it was not a closed circle. Despite expressed fears that the new world was already giving rise to a hereditary nobility lacking only titles, the fact was that there were opportunities for energetic young men, if they were able and lucky enough, to achieve, in time, an upper-class status. Benjamin Franklin was neither rule nor exception in doing so.

The American Revolution split this indigenous ruling aristocracy in two. Those who identified themselves and their interests with English institutions left for Canada or Britain. Those who saw their futures better served by an independent America led the Revolution and then governed the new nation. The Revolution involved no class upheaval, as did the French Revolution some quarter century later. As Dexter Perkins observed, it was a conservative event as far as internal matters were concerned. The upper class—the "aristocracy"—which had functioned as a natural leadership preceding the Revolution continued that function following it, simply reduced in number by those who had fled because of loyalty to Britain.

This Revolutionary bifurcation of the American upper class had the effect of leaving the social and political power structure in the hands of those who, although distinguished by class and wealth, were more individualistic in temperament, philosophically more liberty-oriented, and more opportunistic in action. They had demonstrated a business acumen, but they were not dedicated only to the art of fortune-building. Along with their economic interests they had interests in religion and philosophy, science and literature. They held public office—administrative, legislative, diplomatic, and military; wrote works which are still referred to by scholars, statesmen, and jurists; designed buildings; conducted experiments; and still found time to apply their reason to the improvement of the administration of their agricultural and mercantile enterprises. As products of the Age of Enlightenment, they pursued a life of balance. They constituted, as much as has perhaps ever been achieved, that "natural aristocracy" which some of their number (John Adams, in particular) believed necessary for a good society.

It would be a mistake to view this American leadership of the late eighteenth century as a leisured, intellectual, patrician class. If they were reflective, they were also amazingly vigorous and productive in their own affairs. If they engaged in protracted philosophical dis-

THE ISSUE OF VALUES

course, they were also never-endingly concerned with the economic development of the country they had helped to found. The Protestant fervor for self-improvement ran strong in them.

It would also be a mistake to regard them as the natural leaders of an integrated society. In the first few decades after Independence, the population inland from the Atlantic seaboard, dispersed along a wide frontier, was only loosely linked to the settled East. Aggressively independent and largely self-sufficient, this inland population was not much concerned with national government. In the words of John James Audubon, "An axe, a couple of horses, and a heavy rifle, with store of ammunition, were all that were considered necessary for the equipment of the man, who, with his family, removed to the new state, assured that, in the land of exuberant fertility, he could not fail to provide amply for all his wants." [2] Only occasionally, when federal policy rubbed abrasively, would the West erupt in dissent, as in the Whisky Rebellion of 1794, which President Washington crushed ruthlessly. Otherwise the East went its way, under the leadership of its native aristocracy, and the moving frontier went its ruder way without much leadership of any kind.

In the years after 1800, there were several streams of influence at work which profoundly changed this plastic state of affairs, giving American society sharper definition and providing it with a leadership more suited to a popular following. Of greatest importance was the increase in economic opportunity which followed the earlier period of slow development. In the terminology of our day, the country had reached the stage of take-off into sustained growth. In part this was due to the release of British restrictions on trade and manufacture and the added impetus to local enterprise provided by the disruptions of the Napoleonic war. In part it reflected a phenomenal expansion of internal transportation, especially canals and railroads. Michel Chevalier, the young French engineer who visited the United States in 1833–1835, reported with undisguised admiration that this "movement goes on with increasing speed; the whole country is covered in every direction." [3] Out of this came the geographical expansion of the market. Eastern shops produced for quick

26

sale to interior centers, competing against each other by shaving costs through greater specialization in both the products they sold and the processes by which they made those products. The moving West became more closely integrated with the industrially expanding East. A surge of immigrants, especially Irish and Germans, increased the pool of both consumers and labor.

A second major influence in molding the new nation was a rising egalitarianism. Partly a reaction against the presumed aristocratic pretensions of the old eastern families (as reflected in the fortunes of the Federalist party, which was badly defeated in the election of 1800), it was also in part the French Revolution's recharging of native democratic instincts. Movements in the several states for abolition of property-holder or taxpayer status in order to vote, along with the admission of new states formed out of the western territories, considerably expanded the electorate. With economic development after the War of 1812, western influence in national affairs became more evident. New leaders arose in the West, notably Andrew Jackson and William Henry Harrison, who contrasted sharply with the eastern style. Jackson's election in 1828 was symbolic of "grass roots democracy," combining the denigration of birth and breeding and the exaltation of the common man. Indeed, some historians have claimed that the Jacksonian era represents the high tide of equality of condition and opportunity in the United States, never before—nor since—realized to the same degree.

The spread of economic opportunity and the open access to it gave rise to a new class of thrusters, economic adventurers with a single-minded pursuit of wealth. Obviously there had been individuals of such a bent in Colonial times, but not until the years after 1815 had they set the tone for the nation. If the natural aristocrats of the eighteenth century, apostles of a balanced way of life, were eminently fitted for the founding of a new nation, they were distinctly unsuited to lead a nation of egalitarian-minded devotees of the dollar. "Balance" is too exotic a focal value to be pursued by a whole population, at least for long. Commercial advantage is a passion which more readily activates a nation of individualists, as Tocqueville observed in 1835 after his first visit to the United States. And such a view of man's chief aim and delight could be given respected justification in the belief, brought over from England and assiduously cultivated in a society that combined religious piety with economic development, that an industrious life is a moral life, and economic advancement is a reward from heaven.

The evident success of this new entrepreneurial class, more aggressive and assertive than the old aristocracy, gave rise to the cult of the self-made man. This concept so captured native imaginations that it never quite lost its hold until the Great Depression of the 1930s, despite a waning belief in it in the half-century before that economic cataclysm. E. Digby Baltzell, writing of upper-class society in Philadelphia, comments that after the War of 1812 the genteel drawing rooms of the old aristocracy were penetrated by the new spirit of business adventure, and the founders of new family firms in manufacturing, mining, banking, and transportation were, over the next fifty years, gradually assimilated into the "proper" society of the older order.

The members of that older order had been in the thick of the political activity of their time, writing constitutions, holding public office, and serving abroad as representatives of the new nation. On a lesser scale, the businessmen in the expanding cities of that same period, in the West as well as in the East, had held themselves responsible for civic order and welfare, participating actively in local political life, occasionally, but not always, with their own personal advantage in view. All this changed with the new breed of business thrusters. Concentrating their full attention on the task of making money, they had neither the time nor inclination for public affairs. These they left to another new breed that was springing up alongside of and complementing them—the professional politicians.

If, as Clement Eaton comments, these political leaders of the new era were somehow "less admirable" than the public leaders of the aristocratic period, they were at the same time "much closer to the common man in their thinking." [4] They also fulfilled a different function. The older leaders had wielded an almost independent power. The new politicians were brokers of power, reconciling as best they could popular majorities (under the expanded franchise) and the special interests of the rising business class which was propelling the economy forward with demoniac energy.

These two new breeds, the single-minded businessman and the professional politician, were both creatures of the two streams of influence coalescing in this period—expanded economic opportunity and a surging egalitarian fervor. But the egalitarian movement, in part an objective condition making possible the competitive advancement of those with advantage, skill, daring, and luck, was also partly created by the rising entrepreneurial class which, disdaining conservative sympathy for an anachronistic way of life, most benefited from a society free of entrenched privileges. The egalitarian movement was also partly a response by "the common man," avid for self-advancement, to the conditions being created by the entrepreneurial development of new economic opportunities. The time had not yet come when business interests would be conceived as antagonistic to populist causes. In the heady days of expanding economic opportunity for the masses, the new self-made businessmen were seen as champions of the popular cause, in contrast to the eastern aristocratic families whose contemporary members were viewed as inheritors of privilege. The fight over the renewal of the charter of the second Bank of the United States, opposed viciously by Jackson and his adherents, was regarded as a contest between the forces of democracy and of eastern privilege, the latter personified in the bank's president, Nicholas Biddle of Philadelphia.

If the Jacksonian "revolution" is the high tide of the egalitarian movement, this implies a subsequent recession from that farthest advance. If the two streams of influence—the expanding economy and the expanding electorate—served both business and the common man in this pre-Civil War period, the two streams were already dividing in the beneficence of their effect, already beginning to widen the gap between mass and upper class. The spoils of political office were the rights of the triumphant western "barbarians" over the eastern aristocracy, but this was a small price for the latter to pay for the greater economic prizes which the times were creating. The waves of the Jacksonian revolution washed over, without disturbing, the upper-class eastern business establishment founded on old mercantile and landed fortunes; and numbers of the new "self-made" business leaders likewise rode those same waves to positions of great wealth and power.

The chief opposition to the new business class came not from the ranks of northern democracy but from the southern aristocracy. Old South leaders had had a spiritual kinship with the natural aristocracy of New England and the middle states in the years of the Revolution and the country's founding. Washington was, after all, a Virginia gentleman, his father a planter. But as the North of the early nineteenth century became more commercial, the South became more alienated. If the Northern upper class abandoned balance for a more obsessive pursuit of profit, the Southern upper class dramatized the difference between them by a fanatical devotion to a "balance" which became more exotic and arcane. If the cult of the self-made man flourished in the competitive North, the cult of chivalry and heraldry characterized the semi-feudal South. In *The Fathers,* Allen Tate has vividly described a Virginia tournament of the times, conducted with all the pageantry and trappings of a medieval court. If egalitarian sentiment swept through the North and the frontier West, the institution of slavery—which many old South leaders in the eighteenth century had hoped would disappear in time—became more deeply entrenched than ever. This occurred, in part, because fear of slave insurrections drove southern slaveowners in the nineteenth century to assert the master's role more firmly. A southern middle class of artisans and traders was expanding in number, it is true, but there was little room for their ambitions to expand in a plantation-oriented economy, and attitudes compatible with free labor did not spring naturally within a society that believed in benevolent, but firm, paternalism. C. Vann Woodward makes the essential point: "Far more than an economic relationship, slavery was indeed a way of life and a way of looking at life and the world." [5]

Two such disparate societies could not (at least *historically* could not) effect a viable if implicit bargain on the basis of which they could erect common institutions. As the northern economic thrusters expanded their operations and as the economic opportunities which they were creating attracted from overseas an increasing number of an impoverished or oppressed proletariat, the interests of the two societies diverged more and more sharply. Patched-up compromises proved necessarily unstable. It was reasonable for the South to con- clude that its way of life could be preserved only by separating from the union. Since the North would not permit such self-determination, war was the consequence.

The defeat of the South gave control of its state governments and its economy to the national government, that is, to the victorious North, where the interests of business—nurtured in significant mea- sure by the war itself—were identified with national interest. The South became a conquered territory, to be exploited as such. After twelve years of occupation, it was ready to make a deal. In the disputed presidential election of 1876, Southern support was given to Rutherford B. Hayes, who then withdrew the last of the federal troops upholding the imposed reconstruction governments. The ef- fect of this "Compromise of 1877" was to leave control of the economy of the South largely in the hands of Northern interests, while political control reverted to the South. Southerners became not only the elected representatives of the white electorate, but also the appointed managers and supervisors of Northern-owned businesses.

The end of the Civil War dried up a market which had kept many small, and many new, firms afloat. There ensued a period of merger and consolidation. But what contributed more than any other single factor to the growth in the size of business corporations was the rise of a genuinely national market, symbolized by completion of the first transcontinental railroad in 1864. Indeed, the last third of the nine- teenth century can almost be considered the Age of Railroads, so great was their influence. As the first large-scale, complex, business organizations, they set a pattern for the rationalization of administra- tive management. With their insatiable demand for investment funds, they helped to create a more orderly and permanent network of capital markets and financial managers. With a public-imposed responsibility to remain in operation despite losses due to fiscal irresponsibility or excessive competition, they gave rise to new legal instruments for reconciling social need and investor claims—and in the process gave investment bankers a larger stake in corporate control. With their incredible need for steel for roads which doubled in mileage decade by decade and for rolling stock and river-spanning bridges and terminals and warehouses, they supported almost by themselves the swift growth of the infant steel industry and that industry's rapid increase in productivity, which soon gave it an edge over steel-making in England, from which it had taken its origins.

To coordinate the operations of over a thousand operating railroads into a national network required business cooperation and agreement, the founding of industry associations for self-government, the prodding of state legislatures, and the intervention of the federal government, most notably in the Interstate Commerce Act of 1887. Out of such joint efforts (antagonisms and bargaining leading to eventual collaboration and systematization) came standard gauge tracks, standard time zones to coordinate schedules, and standardization of equipment and operating procedures—through bills of lading, uniform freight classification, and interchange of freight cars.

This physical coupling of regions and producing centers into a single coordinated and immense national market had further repercussions. It encouraged the national corporation, with headquarters and dispersed operations, in contrast to the local family-oriented enterprise. It gave impetus to mass production techniques to supply the expanding market, and made possible, indeed necessary, national advertising of branded products to assure a mass demand sufficient to justify mass production. Scientific management, institutionalized research and development, strategic centralized controls, and somewhat later, sophisticated systems of comprehensive budgeting and planning, all promoted the large business corporation into a position of dominant influence in American society. The educational establishment soon came to service it, most evidently in the founding of the world's first professional schools for the mastery of business administration. Labor unions gave up quixotic notions of restoring a lost society of artisans and accepted the business system of casual wage employment, asking only that they be recognized as part of that system. Governmental acknowledgment of business' central role reached the peak of explicitness in President Calvin Coolidge's simple assertion that "the business of America is business," a statement so compelling in its austerity and sweep that any amendment served only to underscore its validity.

Corporate leadership in the period following the Civil War continued to draw from two quite separate pools, the old aristocratic families and the new self-made men. But the nationalization of the market made a difference. The local aristocracies of the older Eastern cities were amalgamated into a national elite more appropriate to business on a continental scale. The instruments for achieving class solidarity became the exclusive preparatory schools and the Ivy League colleges—Harvard, Yale, and Princeton in particular. Intra-league football (the Big Four included the University of Pennsylvania) was the sport, roughly played, in which the sons of the aristocracy (mostly WASPs) tested their mettle against each other. Dick Friedman has pointed out the sense of racial and ethnic superiority associated with the gridiron supremacy of gentleman-athletes. "The Harvard Club of Boston in 1894 was informed that 'even death on the playground was cheap if it educated boys in the characteristics that had made the Anglo-Saxon race pre-eminent in history." [6] That same aristocratic clannishness was given philosophic expression by a former president of the New Jersey Bell Telephone Company and the Rockefeller Foundation, Chester I. Barnard, who along with Vilfredo Pareto and Elton Mayo (elitists, too), constituted the intellectual trinity to whom the Harvard Business School paid reverence in the period between World War I and World War II. In Barnard's most influential book, *The Functions of the Executive,* he emphasized the importance of the "informal society" of the corporation, based on "communion," which he defined as "personal comfort in social relations," "solidarity," "social integration," "mutual support in personal attitudes." At times, perhaps often, he commented, men cannot be admitted to the corporate hierarchy, not because of lack of competence but because they "do not fit." "Fitness," he observed, involved such attributes as education, race, nationality, faith, politics, sectional antecedents, manners, speech, and personal appearance.[7]

As a consequence of this aristocratic solidarity, the top business leaders at the turn of the century (based on a study of 190 such individuals by William Miller) were "likely" to be of colonial ancestry, from British and New England stock, of the Episcopal, Presbyterian, or Congregational denominations, urban, well educated, from an upper-class family identified with business affairs.[8] Moses Rischin, writing of the same period, concludes that the social patterns within the major corporations "helped to close off key areas of the economy and to keep them virtually impenetrable to even the most gifted outsiders."[9] The U.S. Commission on Industrial Relations in its report in 1915 observed that the bluebloods of industry, occupying only by accident of birth a position "almost exactly analogous to that of feudal lords," held power over the livelihood and happiness of "more people than populated medieval England."

But not all the titans of American business were descendants of colonial families. In the years following the Civil War, as in the years preceding it, the most spectacular successes were such "self-made men" as Andrew Carnegie, Henry C. Frick, John D. Rockefeller, and a little later, Henry Ford. There was an Olympian array of railroad tycoons including Hill, Harriman, Fisk, Gould, and Vanderbilt. Theodore Dreiser said of such "fabulous creatures" that they had become "freaks in the matter of money-getting."[10] Lesser freaks spotted the industrial landscape.

Some without benefit of ancestral name, who managed to make it through one of the preferred colleges, on scholarship or by patronage, were assimilated into the business upper class and allowed to progress part way up the executive ladder of blue-chip corporations. The Eastern collegiate football field became one entree to the world of business privilege. "It was also somehow understood that recruits from a middle-class or lower-class background who achieved stardom were not mongrelizing the game but profiting from contact with their betters. . . . But the methods of advancement were still to be defined on the gentleman's terms and therefore to remain rather exclusive." [11] This was pre-World War I.

Writing of the same period but referring to a somewhat different professional milieu, the historian H. Stuart Hughes provides insights relevant to such assimilated businessmen, "self-made" through educational performance but co-opted on terms dictated by others. He refers to his grandfather, the eminent Chief Justice and presidential candidate, Charles Evans Hughes, whose Welsh father had arrived in New York in 1855 as a destitute immigrant. Having made it through Columbia Law School with distinction, the son was taken up by people of affluence and influence. "Deep down, however, his ascent into the Wasp establishment seems to have taken a great deal out of him. And in two senses: first, in leading him to curb, at least in public, what was volcanic in his own nature; second, in provoking doubt, mostly unconscious, about whether he might not still remain an outsider who was constantly required to prove himself. . . . Like so many other men who have taken a great leap in one generation, he simply assumed the economic system which had made this possible." [12]

America's business leadership in the years before the Great Depression was thus composed in part of a socially integrated, upper-class community, defined by family, educational, and religious boundaries, into which had been recruited able outsiders who had acquired the necessary polish, and also, in part, of a smaller number of aggressive men who had "made it big" on their own but who had not been granted social class standing. This combined leadership had won, for the system on which it thrived, the support of the vast majority of small businessmen and workaday Americans. The dominants of our time, they were the spiritual descendants of the thrusters of a century earlier.

Even those who might have railed against the depredations of "big business" believed that if big business was guilty of sins it was because of its size rather than because of its values. It could and should be controlled but not overturned. Too many people had a stake in it to risk radical social adventuring, even in the depths of the Depression. As Hughes's historian grandson writes of the New Deal Chief Justice, "he was concerned rather with correcting the abuses of a business society than with questioning its fundamentals." [13]

After World War II the makeup of business leadership changed. The large corporation became more than ever its home, but the characteristics of corporate executives became less homogeneous, accommodating a diversity of ethnic background, educational pedigree, and religious affiliation. A number of reasons have been advanced for this deemphasis of class. It has been said that the increasing complexity of technology and even of administration demanded capabilities not always correlated with status. Too much was at stake in the large corporation to make breeding more important than performance in the selection of executives. It has also been argued that the postwar expansion of corporate activity was on too great a scale to limit executive selection to those with class credentials. At least as important, however, was the continuing egalitarian revolution, given renewed impetus by the war itself. In a time of national need, the war provided opportunities for people of all kinds of social backgrounds to prove their skills in leadership, and in its aftermath generated a world-wide wave, leveling all sorts of distinctions based on privilege, particularly on privileges associated with birth, whether familial, ethnic, or racial.

The large American corporation, more impersonal and less a class property, responded more readily to population and political pressures, and selected and socialized its own managers, drawing from a variety of social pools. The "organization man" came from many sources, but the few who made their way to the top were those who accommodated most successfully to corporate requirements. The corporation created its own class, for its own purposes.

This change in the character of business leadership was not associated with any significant change in attitude toward business. However criticized for sins of omission or commission, business remained the most influential institution in American society. Its relations with government showed a clear evolution in one direction—greater interpenetration. In the early decades after the country's founding, business leaders participated in active public life; in the decades up to the Great Depression business leaders, while withdrawing from direct involvement in public affairs, asserted a crude control over legislatures and administrations on the city, state, and federal levels. As Chicago populist, Henry Demarest Lloyd, charged in 1881, "the Standard [Oil Company] has done everything with the Pennsylvania legislature except refine it." [14]

It was, perhaps, about the turn of the century that a few businessmen and observers began to formulate what Lincoln Steffens called a "theory of the unification of business management and political government." This independent and indefatigable journalist-reformer, fresh from disillusioning inquiries into what made Boston run, concluded "that business and politics must be one; that it was natural, inevitable, and—possibly—right that business should—by bribery, corruption, or—somehow get and be the government." [15] His objective, amoral judgment was given a more normative expression by George W. Perkins, former president of the New York Life Insurance Company and a Morgan partner, in a 1908 address at Columbia University. In the conduct of business, said Perkins, the states had become meaningless, while the large corporations had become semipublic national instruments. For the public's benefit, he asserted, the latter should be supervised by individuals who had proved their competence in business administration. "The business man would merge into the public official," who, responding to the responsibilities of office, would become an industrial statesman.

From such a view it is not a long step to John Kenneth Galbraith's "new industrial state" of the 1960s, in which business executives have moved from instinctive opposition to government controls to cooperation in selective controls that will make the system work better. A symbiotic relation emerges between corporations and public agencies, a planning system (even though not discussed as such) in which business is an important participant in the planning. The picture, if drawn with sharp outlines, still elicits protest from most business leaders, who do not recognize their involvement as contributing to such a result (any more than in Lincoln Steffens's day). But if the outlines are blurred just a bit, the picture is more recognizable.

Business leaders are once again active in public life, as in the early nineteenth century. They influence public policy in a variety of ways, some just as crudely as in Vanderbilt's day but most with much subtler, less overweaning methods that involve concessions to critics and accommodation to other interests. So the United States remains a business society—one has only to compare it with other countries to see that. Business leaders, that is, executives of large, mostly financial and industrial corporations, continue to be the dominant influence in American society. But they do so *in their institutional roles* and not as individuals, as in an earlier era. They are dominant not in the sense of having their way in all the things that matter to them, but in the sense of advancing an organization of society and a set of values more acceptable to more people than any competing organization or values.

Nevertheless, the objective conditions affecting American society are undergoing significant changes, testing the capacity of business leaders, as well as the professional politicians who are the brokers of power, to maintain their roles. So far they have done so, chiefly through instruments of concession and co-optation, two of the three means for that purpose. The third, repression, has been less relied on, even though not wholly absent, as investigations into the uses of security organizations, the armed forces, and revenue and credit services have revealed.

It remains to be seen whether business leaders can continue to adapt successfully to ongoing shifts in political, economic, and population movements which are raising rude challenges to the social values which they have advanced and which have advantaged them. Or whether, on the contrary, they may be elbowed aside by some thruster group more capable of viewing those challenges as the conditions for a new society in which their role would expand because it is more needed—a thruster group carrying with it a different set of social values more congruent with the times.

II

EVOLUTION
OF CONTEMPORARY
VALUES

The American
Focal Value

B USINESS, business, business, from morning till night, that is all you see, read, and hear." When he wrote these words in 1876, Henry Sienkiewicz, the Polish author of *Quo Vadis?*, was referring specifically to New York City. However, he extended their application to American society generally. It was, he wrote, "a very one-sided civilization," where it was "the universally accepted opinion . . . that money alone constitutes the worth of a man and that material gains and enjoyment are the sole objectives worth striving for." [1]

Sienkiewicz's view was neither new nor unusual. Tocqueville, almost half a century earlier, had remarked that he knew of no country "where the love of money has taken stronger hold on the affections of men." [2] His fellow-countryman, Chevalier, traveling in the United States at the same time, had similarly observed of "the American" that "his only thought is to subdue the material world. . . . To this sole objective everything is subordinate, education, politics, private and public life." [3]

The pursuit of gain is obviously not solely an American phenomenon. Virtually every philosopher and historian whose writings have survived has commented on its presence and role in human society. What has distinguished the United States is the ubiquity and depth of such passion. It has molded if not preoccupied the thought and actions of most Americans from the nation's beginning. Its hold has increased, not diminished, with the passage of time. At least three reasons jointly account for this conception of what constitutes the chief aim of life.

First, the seventeenth-century colonists were confronted with a degree of economic necessity they had never previously experienced. Provisioning from the old world was too expensive and problematic to rely on. The material base for social existence had to be created out of the resources at hand. Nor was nature so bountiful as in more tropical lands. Economic development was the condition of survival. A work ethic was a matter of necessity. Regardless of status or background the rule was, "he who does not work shall not eat."

But, second, a work ethic was also a matter of election. The Protestant-Puritan creed, in its various versions, provided an intellectual and spiritual fortitude in the overcoming of obstacles to material gain. Alan Simpson has distinguished the "right-wing Puritanism" that reproduced (especially in Massachusetts) Calvinist Geneva's supremacy of the saints, from the neutralism of the separationists who sought a privacy of religious expression free of community control (most notably in Rhode Island), and both of these from the left-wing "levellers" whose convictions became embodied in democratic congregationalism.[4] But through all these variations runs the dogma of vocationalism, so vividly expounded by Cotton Mather in 1701.

The "doctrine of the two callings" affirmed that every Christian has a "general calling" to save his soul through religious practice, but equally a "personal calling," an occupation. "That is to say, there should be some *Special Business* and some *Settled Business,* wherein a Christian should for the most part spend the most of his Time; and this, so he may Glorify God, by doing of *Good* for *others,* and getting of *Good* for himself." Mather hammers the point home with the admonition, "Let your *Business* Engross the *most* of Your

Time." [5] As Simpson comments, the Puritan "develops for religious purposes a type of character which can hardly fail to be a worldly success." [6] Moreover, in marked contrast to the material-minded of other societies and other times, the gain-dedicated Puritans and to a degree, by generational transmission, their descendants, pursued their goal with an almost ascetic discipline, embracing standards of (relative) honesty, sobriety, and reliability.

The third significant influence in the identification of material gain as focal value has been the democratic base of American society. Aristocratic traditions encourage a love of the arts; concern for honor; pride in family; attention to manners; a certain opulence; cultivation of learning and the sciences; an obligation of public service. At their best, such traditions combine to make a conscious balance of these the focal value. We have already noted that in the seventeenth and early eighteenth centuries a kind of "natural aristocracy" was present and influential in American society. But such a focal objective is too difficult for most people to pursue. In a society which stresses democratic, popular control, the tendency is to stress that value of which all are capable without any prior training or tradition—making money—and especially is this so in a young society free of class inhibitions and flaunting abundant opportunities for the pursuit of wealth.

By the time of Jackson's administration, the conditions were ripe for accelerated development, and the Jacksonian victory (reflecting extended suffrage and extended western settlement) promised everyone a share in that development. Economic "take-off" and political take-over coincided. The new business enterprisers, distinguished from the "old money" group, were looked on as both the products and champions of democracy. Democracy readily identified itself with materialism, and business (materialism institutionalized) identified itself with democracy. America, as the most democratic of societies, understandably became the most material-minded. Moses Rischin captures the essence of this philosophical reinforcement of the pursuit of gain: "perhaps nowhere else in the world has a seemingly materialistic cult been so uninhibitedly transformed into a transcendental ideal. . . . Even Walt Whitman could write, in *Democratic Vistas,* 'I perceived clearly that the extreme business energy, and this almost maniacal appetite for wealth prevalent in the United States are parts of amelioration and progress, indispensably needed to prepare the very results I demand. My theory includes riches, and the getting of riches.' " [7] Ralph Waldo Emerson, in his essay "Wealth," rhapsodized over the pursuit of wealth. "Man was born to be rich," he wrote, "or inevitably grows rich by the use of his faculties; by the union of thought with nature. Property is an intellectual production."

The opening up of a "new" country, its democratic social and political base, and the discipline of a Puritan work ethic, combined to make work for gain the universal instrument for self-advancement. "From the moment he gets up, the American is at his work, and he is absorbed in it till the hour of sleep," Chevalier wrote in 1835.[8] "Until four or five o'clock in the afternoon practically all the inhabitants of New York, indeed of the entire country, work with feverish zeal to accumulate a fortune," Sienkiewicz observed in 1876.[9]

Throughout most of the nineteenth century, work, assiduous and disciplined, had as its specific objectives, first, the earning of a "living," but, for many, also the accumulation of enough savings to permit a wage-earner to go into farming or business for himself, to become his own boss. For at least a century Benjamin Franklin's "Poor Richard" served as tutor to the nation, and one of his most repeated admonitions was thrift: "A penny saved is a penny earned"; "a man may, if he knows not how to save as he gets, keep his nose all his life to the grindstone." Emerson, the transcendentalist, urged on men generally the precept of the merchant: "absorb and invest." Every person faced the question of whether to spend or whether to invest. To spend for pleasure was the road to ruin. To invest was the means of climbing on to a higher plateau, acquiring power to engage in projects which freed the imagination. "The true thrift is always to spend on the higher plane; to invest and invest, with keener avarice, that he may spend in spiritual creation and not in augmenting animal existence." For Emerson, then, the pursuit of gain was the pursuit of a higher good. If people should "leave off aiming to be rich," he wrote in "Wealth" in 1860, "civilization should be undone."

The urge to earn, to save, to invest, to own one's own business and then to save to re-invest encountered severer obstacles with the spread of mass production and mass marketing towards the end of the nineteenth century. It took more capital and more expertise to run a business. For a while the dream was sustained by the idea of cooperation—the pooling by workers of their savings and skills to run, jointly, an enterprise of their own. The Knights of Labor promoted this philosophy as a means of avoiding "wage slavery." The idea failed, except in agriculture. Nevertheless, it is remarkable how long the dream persisted. In a study of the New Haven, Connecticut labor market just after World War II, Lloyd Reynolds and Joseph Shister found numbers of workers still harboring the hope of putting enough by to go into business for themselves.[10]

As the national market expanded and new technologies stimulated mass production, as more sophisticated forms of business organization and administration developed, and as financiers became more important in the conduct of business, the ideal of saving for investment and re-investment in one's own enterprise became increasingly remote. Many workers, hired by the hour to perform a specialized task, lost the opportunity for developing a variety of skills fitting them to manage even a small operation. The decline of the Knights of Labor, espousing cooperation, and the simultaneous rise of the American Federation of Labor, accepting the wage system and asking only that the wage be a "good" or a "fair" one, reflected a shift in value orientation.

Work still remained central and the ethic of gain remained firmly in place, but the question which Emerson had said confronted every person, whether to spend or invest, was increasingly being answered in terms of spending rather than investing. Large bodies of workers, many unskilled or semi-skilled, many, as immigrants, lacking even a working knowledge of the language, were not the soil in which the idea of owning one's own business could very well germinate. Even persons with training were readier to accept a managerial position in an expanding corporation rather than attempt to "go on their own" in what was becoming a tougher competitive field. Earning to spend, to consume, replaced saving and investment as a focal objective. The good life was measured by the standard of living. Conspicuous consumption and "keeping up with the Joneses" became more common than frugality as the pattern of conduct by which one got ahead.

Even the successful businessman was caught up in the emphasis on consumption. William Dean Howells provided a contemporary fictional portrait in *The Rise of Silas Lapham,* in which the transition from small producer to big spender was etched with acid disapproval. But justification for the shift in focal value was not lacking. The identification of democracy with small business (enterprise for all) was replaced by an identification of democracy with mass production (consumer goods for all). As Joseph Schumpeter was later to point out, the large corporation, with its innovations in product and process, made available to every shop girl the silk stockings which had been a luxury to the first Queen Elizabeth.

The shift from a small-producer to mass-consumer orientation was facilitated by the growth of the advertising industry. Advertisements in newspapers and magazines increased 80 percent in the decade of the eighties and by a third again in the nineties. Total advertising expenditures amounted to 4 percent of national income by 1910. In part this expansion of printed salesmanship was due to the introduction of rotary presses and pulp paper, reducing costs to both publisher and advertiser. But a major factor was also the nationalization of the market, making nationally distributed magazines a much more valuable medium than ever before.

An interesting side-effect was that women became a more potent economic influence. Whereas their role in a producer's world had been limited by tradition and prejudice, their role expanded in a consumer's society. Purchasing was a function to which they could devote more time than their menfolk. Among the results were what one historian, Edward Kirkland, has called "the feminization of

American purchasing,'' and the flowering in the nineties of women's magazines.

Advertising, to be sure, was not new to America. The use of town criers, handbills, and newspaper notices had been part of the earliest business practices. One investigator estimated that as many as eleven million advertisements of all forms appeared in the single year of 1847.[11] Sienkiewicz noted, in 1876, that enterprising New York businessmen seized on every advantage to post handbills, even to the extent of plastering them on the carcasses of dead animals lying in the streets. But such local and opportunistic publicity was a far cry from the systematic, organized advertising campaigns which now operated on a vaster scale. At the same time Sienkiewicz was noting the peculiar lengths to which aggressive city merchants would go in calling attention to their goods, the *Nation* observed that ''the preparation and planning of advertisements of all sorts have assumed the proportions of a business by itself, to which the entire time and thought of a number of men are devoted.'' [12] The chief marshal of the national centennial of the U.S. Constitution, held in Philadelphia in 1887, reported that he had experienced difficulty in preventing the degeneration of the exposition ''into a mere medium for advertising.'' [13]

David M. Potter identified this institutionalization of advertising as a distinctively American invention, and regarded it as ''one of the very limited group of institutions which can properly be called instruments of social control,'' such as church and school. ''What is basic is that advertising, as such, with all its vast power to influence values and conduct, cannot ever lose sight of the fact that it ultimately regards man as a consumer and defines its own mission as one of stimulating him to consume or to desire to consume.'' [14] Though stimulated by the competitive drive of the individual business firm to sell its particular products, advertising's greater significance is in its aggregate effect, surrounding people of all ages, backgrounds, and tastes with a total environment urging them on to spend and consume. In Daniel Boorstin's phrase, advertising is ''the rhetoric of democracy.''

This consumer orientation, abetted by its handmaiden, advertising, creates its own ethic, its own image of the good life. The advertising agent who promotes that life becomes—as much as the producer of goods—esteemed for his contributory role. (In a *New Yorker* cartoon, the artist William Hamilton has an admiring girl leaning across a table for two, saying to the suave young man, "I just love your voice. It's incredibly warm and sincere—honest-sounding. I'll bet you could make a pile doing commercials.") People come to think of themselves in the image of the life that advertising creates for them. (John P. Marquand, in *Point of No Return,* has his young businessman-on-the-rise regarding his attire as he dresses for the office, reflecting to himself: "It was not a bad-looking suit at all and in fact it made him look rather like one of those suburban husbands you often saw in advertising illustrations, a whimsically comical man who peeked naively out of the corners of his eyes at his jolly and amazed little wife who was making that new kind of beaten biscuits.")

Potter, like a number of others, believed that the consumption ethic has a pervasive influence on American culture, particularly on its newspaper and magazine, radio and television content. "The program or the article becomes a kind of advertisement in itself. . . . Its function is to induce people to accept the commercial, just as the commercial's function is to induce them to accept the product." [15] Nor—as is appropriate to the legatee of the Puritan effort—does consumption come painlessly (Bentham was wrong). As Caryl Rivers, analyst of public communications, writes: "The housewives in TV commercials stalk dirt, dust and stale air with the vengeance of Torquemada hunting heresy. The Lysol lady sticks her nose in the sink and sniffs, declaring that her kitchen must smell as good as it looks. The women in the Joy commercials get their dishes so clean guests can see their faces in them, a fact that dominates the dinner conversation. In the world of the commercial, floors gleam like mirrors, dirty T-shirts emerge from the washer as pure as the driven snow, the patina of polished furniture is flawless. Perfection is possible, the ads tell us, and must be striven for; the housewife, in her striving, will stimulate the market for the countless products which are essential for such a search.'' [16]

Consumption as a focal value accepts the devaluation of work. Work loses its quality of fulfilling a human need, its potential for expressing the person (Emerson's investment in self). Work becomes a trade-off for what it will buy. A sustained stream of new or restyled products, along with supportive advertising, insures that the trade-off of devalued work will continue to be forthcoming. One need not be as cynical as Samuel Vauclain of the Baldwin Locomotive Works, who suggested that the automobile had saved the United States from revolution by giving industrial workers ''a glorified rattle'' to keep them occupied, [17] to recognize that the stimulus to consume has given to twentieth-century Americans the closest approach to what classical economists conceived of as an insatiable appetite for goods and services.

This social value has been translated into national purpose. The rate of economic growth (percentage increase in Gross National Product) has become perhaps the single most compelling government objective, without respect to the composition of GNP. The importance of a product in some hierarchy of social need is a concept dismissed as vaguely and excessively subjective, infringing on the individual's tastes and on the consumer's sovereignty. The measure of value is what people will buy. This consumption neutrality has been evidenced by the preference for tax cuts instead of government spending as a means of providing economic stimulation when needed; the former leaves decisions to each consumer, and spreads the benefits among producers accordingly and impartially; the latter requires government intervention in the market, a form of favoritism which undermines competition among producers for the consumer's dollar, and indirectly lessens the overall stimulus to consume.

Careful nourishment of the consumption ethic is essential in order to provide people with jobs; stimulating aggregate demand is recognized as the basis for a healthy economy. People must consume in order to support the production and jobs that provide the income with which to consume. The only alternatives are some form of charitable assistance—welfare payments, subsidized rentals, food stamps, medicaid—or public service jobs. These may be necessary in some degree (indeed, exist only because necessary), as concessions to defuse more radical threats to the prevailing economic system with its preferred values. On too massive a scale, however, they would undercut the existing system, with its emphasis on privacy. Hence the absolute dependence of the dominant business institutions on maintaining a high demand for consumer goods. But hence also the same dependence of labor unions (adjuncts to the corporation, led by men who have learned to benefit their memberships, that is, provide jobs and incomes within the existing system) and of educational, religious, and philanthropic institutions (endowed with assets invested in business corporations, their budgets geared to a sustained level of aggregate consumption).

The focal social value in the United States has thus, since at least the early years of the nineteenth century, reflected that objective conducing most to the advantage of business. This is not because business hoodwinked the public or imposed itself on an unwilling citizenry but because a majority of the public found the value espoused by business very much to its taste. American society found in the idiosyncratic, ebullient entrepreneurial leadership of the nineteenth century, and the efficient, institutionalized corporate leadership of the twentieth century the carriers of a conviction with which they readily identified themselves and their country. That business found suitable instruments for the spread and indoctrination of the focal social value—work and invest for gain, changing to work and consume to get ahead—is no indictment of its purpose or integrity. Any dominant group, in any society, does no less. That there were recurring periods of public doubt concerning the capability and suitability of business leadership does not deny the public's generally acquiescent attitude; no leadership retains the faith of its followers 100 percent of the time.

6

The American
Constitutional Value

THE AMERICAN constitutional value is easier to define than it is to explain. The source of any coercive action in support of the social order lies ultimately in the people themselves—self-government. The application of coercive power is to be strictly limited, respecting the rights of the individual (individualism) and relying as much as possible on private initiative to meet society's needs and wants (laissez faire).

In a detailed study of western societies between 1760 and 1800 R. R. Palmer identifies the "idea of the people as a constituent power," from which the government derives its legitimacy, as the "truly revolutionary" contribution of the new United States. In Europe before the French Revolution, the power of the governing aristocracies was growing stronger. "Everywhere, except in the United States, the problem of taking wider classes of people into the community was either not recognized as a problem, or was plainly denied to be a problem, or was unsolved."

In the American scheme, there were to be two levels of law: the higher law or constitution, which only the people could make or modify through procedures prescribed by their direct representatives, and a second level consisting of legislative law limited to those spheres permitted by the higher law. "All government was limited government," subject to the power of the people in their constitutional role.[1] The French visitor, Chevalier, in 1833, observed that "self-government is the only form of government to which the American character, as it is, can accommodate itself." [2]

Even in the American scheme there were limits to a truly "popular" government; the franchise, for example, was not extended to all, not even to all adult white males. A number of states imposed property qualifications, the last of which, in Rhode Island, was not removed until after the Dorr rebellion in 1843. Justification for restricting the vote to those with some property undoubtedly rested partly on the Burkean pragmatic conviction that those with a stake in the social system would be less disposed to radical political beliefs; more philosophically, though, the correlative principle held that some property was necessary for independence of judgment, since a needy citizen would be too prone to listen to the economic seductions of a demagogue.

Self-government, that is, government by mutual consent, had its roots in the Enlightenment faith that each individual was best able to cultivate his own interests, accountable to himself for himself. But Enlightenment faith went beyond a simple self-serving principle. It conceived of the individual as an inquiring and freethinking, also moral and responsible, unit of society. Self-government implied a contribution to, not separation from, the community of which the individual was a part. Individualism was both the necessary condition for, and the consequence of, self-government. Only he that ruled himself was likewise capable of joining in civic government—Proverbs 16:32—but everyone was said to have that capability. Individualism was both an ideal and a constitutional reality.

This concept of individualism, like that of self-government, found its political expression in the United States. The founding fathers were themselves children, some, indeed, brothers of the Enlightenment. They embedded the idea of a protected sphere of personal activity removed from the oversight of government in the Bill of

The American Constitutional Value

Rights. The self-interests that these natural aristocrats sought to safe-guard were not narrowly conceived. They extended, expansively, to social, intellectual, and convictional matters, beliefs, idiosyncracies, and freedom from arbitrary interventions of search or seizure or censorship.

The specifically economic aspects of self-interest were singularly provided for in the companion concept of private initiative, or *laissez faire*. According to this concept, the enterprising individual advanced himself materially through his own exertion and daring, and the property which he acquired by mingling his labor with nature's resources (where was the Lockean language more appropriate?) was protected to him by the state. Such protection was indeed (again Locke) the chief function of established government, not because property rights were paramount to all other values but because they were essential to independent self-government, the constituent authority. Similarly, if individual initiative was to be encouraged, then the freedom and sanctity of voluntary contracts must be assured. Mutual consent was the basis for *both* private contract and social contract, and for private relationships and public associations. Such contractual undertakings, the private and public expressions of self-government, must both be conceived as immune from any arbitrary acts of legislature.

The four pieces of the constitutional value fitted together snugly—individualism, laissez faire, private property, and freedom of contract. Certain areas of ambiguity were to emerge and be clarified by controversy. If government powers were limited, if private initiative was to be preferred, did this disbar government from affirmative economic action? The answer, hammered out in specific situations (purchases of territory, programs for transportation facilities, agricultural research), seemed to be that government could facilitate private initiative or take initiatives which lay beyond private capacities, but it was not to preempt private initiative. If private initiative and contract were to be encouraged and protected, were there then *no* limits on private actions, even though public actions were held within limits? Again, through confrontation of specific situations, the principle

53

seemed to emerge that when the purpose of private actions was to injure others and deny them equal freedom of action, or when the injurious effect of private action was markedly disproportionate to the gain sought, private actions could be inhibited and private agreements struck down.

Once embedded in political document and subjected to the necessity of transformation into practice, with all the compromises and concessions that politics requires, the philosophical luster of any constitutional value is bound to acquire tarnish. With the passing of the natural aristocracy, the expansion of business activity, and the extension of suffrage, individualism took on more and more of an economic connotation. By the time of Tocqueville's visit, freedom of thought and expression—so important an ingredient in the individualism conceived by the recognized leaders in the years before 1815—were severely restrained by truculent popular opinion, and the Frenchman could remark that he knew of no country so intolerant of controversial views. "In America the majority raises formidable barriers around the liberty of opinion; within these barriers an author may write what he pleases, but woe to him if he goes beyond them." [3]

His countryman, Chevalier, writing at the same time, commented to the same effect. The absence of governmental restraint should not be confused with the absence of all restraint. If liberty was measured by "the number of actions that are permitted or tolerated in public and private life," the advantage lay with old Europe. The reason for this, he believed, was that the Virginian (chiefly Jeffersonian) view of individualism—more open options, more varied tastes, greater breadth of interest—had been eroded by the time of the Jacksonian democratic revolution. "It is the Yankee who now rules the Union; it is his liberty which has given its principal features to the model of American liberty." And of this New England breed, going back to colonial days, Chevalier notes: "The Yankee type exhibits little variety; all Yankees seem to be cast in the same mold; it was, therefore, very easy for them to organize a system of liberty for themselves, that is, to construct a frame within which they should have the necessary freedom of motion." [4]

The more balanced focal value of the earlier natural aristocracy, Northern as well as Southern, had already been displaced by a more monolithic and democratic focal value emphasizing material gain. Entrepreneurial business leadership was asserting itself, winning a wider following than the descendants of the colonial upper class. In the process the concept of individualism became modified—less concerned with matters social and intellectual, which were devalued as Tocqueville and Chevalier testify at an early stage of this development, and more concerned with the purely economic. Individualism and private initiative tended to fold into one, "free enterprise" subsuming both; the heroic figure was no longer the statesman-intellectual-man of affairs but the self-made man.

The correlation between economic individualism and private enterprise was relatively good in the days when most businesses were small and many individuals could reasonably hope to start or own one. The United States of the first half of the nineteenth century was—more than any other western society—a nation of small producers.[5] As the century wore on, however, the transportation network spread, markets and the scale of enterprise expanded, finance capitalism underwrote mergers and acquisitions, and corporation lawyers developed new instruments of control (the trust, the pool, later the holding company). The correlation between economic individualism and private enterprise lost its generality as private enterprise divided into the small, local firm (whether farm, business, or profession) and the still few but increasingly important expanding national corporations. The latter came to seem an antagonist of the former.

The last half of the nineteenth century saw the rise of the Grangers, Populists, Anti-monopolists, Greenbackers, and other similar movements, all urging legislation designed to curb oppressive corporate practices. These movements did not attack either the focal material value or the constitutional values of self-government

and individualism. Edward C. Kirkland, writing of three of the leading reformers of this period, Henry George, Edward Bellamy, and
Henry Demarest Lloyd, notes that all three "reflected American insistence upon efficiency and upon production, pride in national
greatness based on productivity, belief in natural law, preference for
'economy' in government and mistrust of 'restrictive' governmental
legislation." [6] When the Chicago Civic Federation convened a Conference on Trusts in 1899, its "consistent theme . . . was that The
Standard [Oil Company] had driven out of business producers who
wanted to stay in business." A Cornell professor of economics expounded to approving conferees that (in Kirkland's paraphrase)
"every man should have a business and the right to succeed in it (a
sort of homestead thinking applied to industry)." [7]

The threat to individualism from large-scale operation came also
on another front. Mass production was fragmenting the skills of artisans and journeymen and assigning pieces of their former skills as
routines to unskilled immigrants, women, and children. The National Labor Union and the Knights of Labor never wearied of sing-
ing this theme. Before long, scientific management would introduce
time and motion study into the shop, standardizing operations
and establishing production quotas. The possibility of graduating to
self-employment became increasingly remote for the average
wage-worker. Individualism, particularly in the economic sense
it had come to have, seemed a casualty of expanding corporate
organization.

Exercising their presumed rights of self-government, majorities in
a number of states elected legislatures which passed laws curbing
some of the protested abuses of big business, notably in the fields of
minimum wages and maximum hours, forms of wage payment, child
labor, and utility pricing. But most such legislation fell afoul of the
constitutional principle embedded in the American conception of
self-government, that two-level system of law which subordinated
legislatures to the constituent power of the people themselves, expressed in the Constitution and designed to protect the individual.
Federal courts for seventy years, from the mid-sixties of the nine-

teenth century to the mid-thirties of the twentieth century, with few exceptions, struck down such state laws (and federal laws on the same matters) as government interferences with protected private rights. Legislatures had abridged the constitutional freedom to contract (of an employee with an employer, for example, the employee should be free to sell his labor for whatever he thought in his best interest, and the employer similarly to set the terms on which he was willing to hire labor); legislatures had deprived citizens of the rights of property without due process (for example, by control over rates and prices). Attempts to justify such actions by the assumed "police powers" of government to protect the health and welfare of citizens were overridden by the constitutional principle. "To sustain the individual freedom of action contemplated by the Constitution, is not to strike down the common good but to exalt it," the Supreme Court said as late as 1923, in condemning minimum wage legislation, "for surely the good of society as a whole cannot be better served than by the preservation against arbitrary restraint of the liberties of its constituent members."

Federal legislation restricting the anti-competitive and discriminatory business practices of big business was handled less roughly by the federal courts, but even when surviving the constitutional test such legislation was administered with leniency by regulatory agencies and interpreted narrowly by the judiciary. In effect, the courts extended to corporations, as fictive persons, regardless of their size and power, the same protected rights that a natural person enjoyed. In matters affecting competition, this construction ran counter to the interests of the small businessman and farmer and the professional person, who would have preferred to curb the corporation's power. But these same groups found the judicial reasoning reassuring and compelling when it struck down legislation—and union pressures— which would have limited their own freedom in labor matters. If the community's interests were conceived to lie in the avoidance of monopoly powers and the maintenance of personal liberties, this philosophy could be directed against union organization, which exploited the community by wage exactions and strikes and deprived workers of their individual rights. And it was the large corporations which could most successfully carry such complaints through the courts, right up to the Supreme Court, if necessary, with the result that down to 1935 an imposing structure of judicial precedents circumscribed union behavior, to the advantage of the small employer as well as the giants.

It was likewise with the major business interests, especially industrial and financial, that leadership rested in the protracted struggle against a tax on incomes, again benefiting others with smaller stakes to defend. Thus the population of large corporations did not find itself isolated from all other segments of American society, but instead gathered under its patronage, almost without effort and often without gratitude, a growing middle-class population which found the constitutional values of individualism and private initiative a protection against a democratic mass which might exploit them. Protection of rights of property and contract—the individualist credo—ran to the benefit of those who had anything to protect. In the words of David J. Brewer, Justice of the U.S. Supreme Court, in an address before the American Bar Association in 1893, "Here there is no monarch threatening trespass upon the individual. The danger is from the multitudes—the majority, with whom is the power." [8]

With the twentieth century came the organizational revolution, the transformation of the United States from a nation still reflecting a large element of individualistic philosophy and activity to a nation whose life became organized around institutions, with their attendant bureaucracies. With business as the dominant functional category, the expanding and proliferating corporations led the way in effecting this transformation. They drew into themselves activities which had formerly been contracted out, centralizing functions (like personnel administration) which had previously been left in the hands of shop supervisors or plant managers. They integrated what had been local family firms into a national network, promoting their names, trademarks, and slogans into a pantheon of forces molding the lives and fortunes of the population. They extended their activities abroad in a developing pattern of multinational operations. With these and other actions, the large corporations achieved a more impersonal and more institutional leadership role than their predecessors of the previous century. The "Fortune 500"—the annual honors list, in terms of size, compiled by America's most prestigious business publication— would have been inconceivable fifty years earlier.

Around the large corporations orbited their satellites—institutions accommodating to the corporations' unique and central role, changing their own organizational forms and aspirations to keep in step with the business leaders. Labor organization spread from World War I on. For a time the growth came largely in company unions, but after the New Deal it came in independent unions, which expanded, merged, centralized, and bureaucratized like the corporations which were their reason for being. Nonprofit institutions—educational, religious, philanthropic—provided cultural functions and services on an increasingly organized and regularized basis, their business-oriented and business-like administration reflected in the composition of their supervising boards, which were graced by the presence of corporate officials.

Government itself followed the corporate lead. President Warren G. Harding spoke for the nation when he asserted, "We want a period in America with less government in business and more business in government" (a return to *normalcy*). "Every principle and device which promotes efficiency in private business should be adapted and applied in government affairs." [9] Even in Woodrow Wilson's time, though more so during the presidential terms of Harding and Coolidge, electorates in the swelling cities were turning to "city managers" as a means of coping with urban problems in a more efficient, business-like manner. Writing in the early days of the Harding administration, James Harvey Robinson of the New School for Social Research observed that "business indeed has almost become our religion." [10]

This organizational revolution necessitated a reinterpretation of the constitutional values of self-government, individualism, and private enterprise. Self-government continued to emphasize restraint on governmental initiatives, enforced through judicial review (a peculiar process, conservative in effect, but essential to the idea of the people as the constituent political power). Private initiative was interpreted as whatever was nonpublic, a condition fulfilled by the large corporation no less than by its satellite rings of small businessmen supplying it with materials, and selling and servicing its products. Large areas of organized, but private, activity were thus left outside the area of public control. The free initiative of a General Motors or a U.S. Steel was as protected as the free initiative of a candy store.

The historical continuity of this preference for private over public initiatives, regardless of the changed organizational form of the private source, was emphasized in 1923 when the newly formed American Law Institute (representative of bench, bar, and academy) undertook to clarify legal thinking by a series of "Restatements of the Law." These were designed as definitive summations of legal principles governing certain kinds of relations, notably those pertaining to property and contract. A common attitude prevailed among the collaborators. "Confident that laissez faire would yield the greatest good for the greatest number, both groups [academics and practitioners] sought to facilitate the voluntary transactions of free individuals within a legal framework that hindered private initiative as little as possible." [11]

If private initiative was still to be relied on, laissez faire was a weaker reed. The latter was not a necessary corollary of the former. The Great Depression followed by World War II demonstrated that the purposes of a large nation could not be fully realized by as large a measure of governmental nonintervention as had earlier been the case. Nevertheless, the government's role could still be largely confined to regulation and coordination. There was only a limited need for public initiative—nuclear energy at the start (but with strong pressures early developing to turn it over to the private sector), satellite launchings (but with private business collaboration). In most other areas government could subsidize or contract for the private enterprise's efforts. But, after Herbert Hoover's administration, its role as guarantor of the nation's economic health could not be contracted out. And after Franklin D. Roosevelt, the government was not only doctor, prescribing treatment to alleviate distress, but manager, prescribing the conditions to maintain economic equilibrium—first, full employment, later, price stability as well.

The heightened reliance on government as regulator and coordinator of the economic system as a whole does of course chip away some of the corporation's autonomy. It does so, however, to preserve the larger autonomy which remains to the private sector. While the corporate community may continue to complain of government intervention, its complaints are less insistent. It has itself become largely persuaded, almost against its will, of the need for greater governmental coordination if the economy—which is the base of its power—is to prosper. Moreover, private business still remains the strongest influence on national policy. If its organizational autonomy has been attenuated, this has been necessary for the reinforcement of its position. Private initiative may be less private and less independent than formerly, and *laissez faire* now more often *laissons nous,* but the constitutional principles of private property and contract, and the discretion still inhering in them, become more tenable as a consequence.

Like private initiative, the concept of individualism has also had to undergo reinterpretation in the face of the organizational revolution. Whereas the nineteenth century had stressed the individual as his own master, even in the face of changes which made that value ever harder to achieve, the twentieth century more frankly abandoned this conception, as suited only to a simpler society. As individuals came to accept, out of necessity, the fact that the lives of most of them would be spent as employees of an institution, adapting to bureaucratic disciplines, individualism gradually acquired a different meaning. An honored value, built into the national identity and so incorporated into the identity of its members, could not easily be abandoned, but it could be altered to fit the changed circumstances. Individualism became the freedom of any person to make his fortune within the organizational world as well, though less realistically, as in the world outside it.

61

No restraints prevented the individual from changing jobs, changing neighborhoods, changing occupations, or changing regional location in his upward climb toward material achievement. If his fortune was to be made in a large corporation rather than in an enterprise of his own, it remained up to him—and within his grasp—to advance himself by all the effort, skill, and competitive artifice which earlier individualists had employed in trying to make their way independently. Individualism could thus be stretched to include the "organization man," whose number grew so steadily that he became the representative American. The inner-directed man of a younger society—autonomous, self-disciplined, the center of a world he made for himself—gave way to Riesman's other-directed man, responsive to the authority of a larger social system in which he played a small functional part, but still a part to which he gravitated on his own rather than was assigned.

The large corporation which had intruded so rudely into the American scene at the turn of the century and had appeared to threaten its constitutional values had by midcentury become a familiar part of the landscape, and no longer seemed such a threat. It provided careers for many if not most of the graduates turned out by the numerous schools of business administration (the very term signaled a shift from earlier days when business was more entrepreneurial). Its brand names conveyed an assurance of product quality to masses of consumers. It became one of the principal purveyors of culture through its sponsorship of television programs, museum exhibitions, and musical performances. Its buildings dominated urban skylines, often contributing whatever architectural distinction was to be found there. The growing sophistication of corporate public relations activities helped to give big business a more "human" image.

With familiarity came acceptance. In 1964 Richard Hofstadter could ask, "Whatever happened to the anti-trust movement?" and answer his own question by saying that it had ceased being a populist cause and had become institutionalized and bureaucratized in government. An Anti-Trust Division carried on its work routinely, but people at large were no longer worried about bigness. Indeed, it could be argued that the large corporations were simply proportioned to a larger nation.

Nevertheless, there were problems presented by the change in scale. The large corporations, private though they were, themselves exercised significant coercive authority over large blocs of employees, suppliers, agents, and consumers. Some scholars (notably A. A. Berle) argued the necessity of a bill of rights and a due process clause protecting individuals against abuse by big firms, not because corporate managements were malevolent but because their influence was so extensive and so often infused with powers of agency on behalf of the government itself that they could do injury to individual citizens even without intent, indeed in the very process of engaging in actions intended for the common good. In abandoning a pollution-causing plant, they could bring economic hardship on an entire community; in agreeing to seniority ladders in response to union urging, they could freeze out blacks from the better jobs; in protecting the security of military weapons being built within their plants, they could blacken the reputation of individuals failing to pass the security tests; in protecting the reputation of the company they could infringe on the freedom of employees outside working hours. Their private status thus offered no protection against jeopardy to others' private rights.

Discretion in the use of power, however justified, however well intentioned, could be misguided. Private authority on so large a scale could infringe on others' rights, without recourse by those injured, unless the power of government was used to impose constitutional limitations on it: the need for regulation presented itself again. Hence the succession of laws, beginning with the labor legislation of the thirties, and expanded in the civil and economic rights legislation of the 1960s and 1970s, subjecting private initiative to certain legal constraints and curbing the coercive power, particularly of business, over private citizens. No longer could business discriminate against individuals because they joined labor unions, or because they were black, or female, or old, even if such actions had been undertaken impersonally rather than vindictively, for reasons of business efficiency, in the spirit of Chester Barnard. No longer could the large national, mass-producing corporations so easily palliate the protests of consumers who felt exploited by poor performance, or unenforceable warranties, or hazards to health or safety (a kind of denial of an implicit contractual relationship), or the complaints of groups or communities whose environments were polluted or despoiled (a kind of deprivation of property without due process).

From the standpoint of regulated business, such governmental interventions can be construed as interference with their private initiative. From the standpoint of those protected, the limitations on the private power of business are the necessary correlatives of the safeguarding of their own private rights and freedom of action. From the standpoint of society as a whole, the modifications in the discretionary authority of business are changes in the implicit bargain, whose terms are always being renegotiated, through the mediation of the professional politicians, enabling the value structure to survive even if in altered form.

In overall assessment, America's constitutional value continues to stress self-government as both the power of the people to originate their own form of government, and a restriction of the power of government to those areas authorized by the constituent people. This limitation on the powers of transitory governments to legislate in spheres unauthorized by the more permanent, constitutional authority continues to serve a conservative function, but massed political pressures make it less protective of property and contractual rights than formerly. Private initiative continues to be given preferred status, but with languishing benefit from laissez faire. Individualism, still primarily conceived as an economic matter, is increasingly concerned with the status of individuals within large organizations, the freedom and privacy of the organization man and woman. Right of private initiative notwithstanding, large-scale organizations are thus drawn more directly into the framework of social sanctions respecting the uses of coercive power. Their actions, less than but like the actions of government, are constrained by the very constitutional value which constrains the actions of government itself vis-a-vis them. In the words of Alpheus T. Mason, circumstances have "transmuted the issue of liberty versus authority into the problem of responsible use of power—the power of individuals and groups as well as of official government." [12]

7

The American
Distributive Value

AMERICAN VIEWS as to how the benefits of their society
should be distributed have centered around the idea of equality, but
the meaning of that term has been peculiarly elusive. It has been
most commonly used to refer to equality of opportunity, but even
that usage is opaque. The idea of equality clearly involved, from earliest colonial days, the rejection of the view that an inherited or
ascribed status enjoyed special privileges. This meant no formal aristocracy, equality before the law, general suffrage (property qualifications did exist but were not prohibitive to large numbers of the
working population), freedom of occupational pursuit, and, above
all, the right to acquire and enjoy wealth.

Within this broad compound of beliefs, on which there was general agreement, there was considerable room for disagreement.
Some worried that the idea of equality could be carried too far, leading common men without education or experience to consider themselves as "good" as society's most enlightened citizens. The dis-
avowal of inherited inequalities did not rule out the existence of
natural inequalities of talent and intellect, as John Adams wrote to
Jefferson in the days of their retirement, and a society which did not

make provision for such a natural aristocracy to guide its fortunes was setting up conditions for a moneyed aristocracy—''land jobbers and stock jobbers''—to take over. Jefferson headed the school of philosophic optimists who readily conceded the existence of a natural aristocracy (after all, Jefferson was foremost in that category) but believed that citizens in free elections, for their own good, would elevate such superior individuals to leadership roles.[1]

Others recognized that equality of opportunity, in any literal sense, was a chimera: classes did exist and could not be wished away, and children born into the upper social class or higher income class obviously enjoyed special advantages. But the equality-optimists satisfied themselves that such advantages, present in a family in one generation, would be lost in the succeeding generation, and vice versa, so that the lottery of fortune prevented any systematic favoritism. Equality of opportunity did not exist among all people at every moment, but was generally present over the long pull.

European visitors throughout the eighteenth and nineteenth centuries, making comparisons with their own countries, were continuingly impressed with the absence of class distinctions, except in the feudal South. Tocqueville made it the pervading theme of his extensive observations. Sienkiewicz assured his readers back home that it was not only theory but practice for men to regard each other as social equals. ''In a word, they do not stand on different rungs of the social ladder, for the simple reason that there is no ladder here at all.'' [2] The widespread respect for work—work of all sorts—was the common leveler. Chevalier, attributing this attitude to the Reformation, whose influence was so marked in American origins and evolution, noted that here work, in all forms, gave abundantly to everyone the material rewards which formerly had been reserved for a few. Sienkiewicz put the matter succinctly: ''How can one look down upon a tavern-keeper, a grocer, or a craftsman who only yesterday was a governor or a senator and who tomorrow, if his party secures a majority and takes over the government, will again occupy an equally important or more important office?'' [3] Numerous Europeans remarked, often with distaste, on the way that men of standing were subjected to back-slapping and gossipy familiarity by people of limited education and breeding.

The European preoccupation with American equality was partly an understandable reaction to the contrast with their own class-oriented societies and partly an imprecise reflection on the general prosperity which they found. But American attitudes on this score were even stronger. Equality *existed* and was to be defended against any suspicion of privilege. Tocqueville and Chevalier both remark on the general intolerance of any show of pomp, which necessitated that those with superior virtues and wealth should not flaunt these lest they excite envy. It was not financial success itself which drew opprobrium—that, after all, was the reward for which everyone was striving. It was the display of wealth or breeding as though these were marks of superiority, when in fact the one might equally accrue to any man through his own efforts, and the other was viewed as false coin. Not success, but a pretense to social distinction excited public animosity.

Equality of opportunity—free access by all to the great economic marketplace—rested first and foremost on the principle of competition, that is, that the good things society produced would be distributed among its members depending on how well they played the game. Rewards would go to those with the greatest native shrewdness, skill, energy, ambition, and persistence. Hard work and daring would pay off in the end, justifying the wealth which anyone acquired by his own efforts—the ideology of the "self-made man." (There were also those with a continuing belief in the "covenant with God," that Calvinist conception that God would reward those who best pursued their vocation.)

Such a philosophy of distribution was highly acceptable to a race of uninhibited wealth-seekers exploiting a new continent. Again we turn to visitors from Europe for testimony as to the fanaticism with which competition was embraced. Chevalier quotes an informant as saying: "An American is always on the lookout lest any of his neighbors should get the start on him. If one hundred Americans were going to be shot, they would contend for first place, so strong is their habit of competition." [4]

The American Distributive Value

The philosophical validation for the competitive principle supplied by classical economists from Adam Smith on was reinforced by social Darwinism, a theory so effectively expounded by Herbert Spencer that historian Russell Nye has evaluated his influence on American thought as probably greater than any philosopher since John Locke. "No authority," writes Nye, "was cited more frequently by economic writers between 1880 and 1890. . . . His name and ideas were by 1890 virtually household words." [5] Spencer, not himself an economist, lent the weight of his authority to an economic version of Darwin's findings, which emerged in the catchy phrase, "survival of the fittest." Who the fittest were was determined by competition, ruthless if need be, since nature had no mercy. The competitive principle was enshrined as a scientific law, immutable, beyond the power of any government to set aside. If competition in the economic sphere led to the demise of many struggling businesses and the survival of a few large firms, this only demonstrated the superiority of the latter within the given social environment, which was both hospitable and hostile to all alike.

Social Darwinism became the philosophic weapon with which to attack government regulation of business even when the latter had been conceded as a result of political (democratic) pressures. Four years after passage of the Interstate Commerce Act, the president of the Union Pacific insisted that rates would still be subject to "the great law of competition." [6] The historian Edward C. Kirkland, after an intensive study of this period, comments that "affirmations of this sort were not merely a handy stick to beat the dog of governmental rate regulation; private communications between railroad men expressed the same dogma." [7]

Indeed, the concept of America as the land of opportunity rested squarely on a belief that its rewards were distributed to all in accordance with the effectiveness of their competition, without respect to family background. If this was a credo congenial to businessmen, it was also endorsed by educators and ministers. "The approved version had powerful support from all segments of society. It had the sanction of the leading American economists; it was taught in all classrooms and permeated all the popular text-books. . . . Among intellectuals, William Graham Sumner was undoubtedly the most commanding and influential of the Spencerians; the only law of business, he told a student at Yale, was 'root hog or die,' " the only sound economic system "was the contract-competition system, all others are fallacies." [8] The novelist John P. Marquand portrayed the cultivation of this idea in younger minds, including many who would never enter Yale or any other collegiate school, in *Point of No Return*. The novel has a candidate for the Massachusetts legislature delivering the graduation address to the Clyde grammar school, his phrases redolent with the accepted truth—"The greatest country in the world," where all men are "free and equal," "you are all starting even because this is America, no matter what may be your religion or race or bank account." And Marquand muses, through his fictional character Charles Gray: "This credo was all a part of the air one breathed in Clyde. Later, if it did not jibe with experience, you still believed. If you heard it often enough, it became an implicit, indestructible foundation for future conduct." [9]

In 1922, then Secretary of Commerce Herbert Hoover, already a respected stateman because of his leadership in American-sponsored relief missions during and after World War I, publicly reaffirmed this "indestructible" concept. American individualism embraced "these great ideals: that while we build our society upon the attainment of the individual, we shall safeguard to every individual an equality of opportunity to take that position in the community to which his intelligence, character, ability, and ambition entitle him; that we shall keep the social solution free from frozen strata of classes; that we shall stimulate effort of each individual to achievement; that through an enlarging sense of responsibility and understanding we shall assist him to this attainment; while he in turn must stand up to the emery wheel of competition." [10] Hoover had these words italicized, the only phrases given such emphasis in the little volume in which they appear.

Despite the vitality and continuity of the principle that competition under conditions of equal opportunity should govern the distribution of society's benefits, and the fierce will to believe that this was so, class distinctions did exist, had indeed existed before the Revolution and continued to exist after the Revolution. If the United States could justifiably pride itself on a condition of general equality far surpassing any European experience, it had by no means achieved a state of classlessness.

Inequality in the United States in the nineteenth and early twentieth centuries took several forms. The most blatant was racial inequality, so transparent that it could be reconciled with American values only by treating blacks and Indians as inferior species, hence not included in any guarantees of open access to opportunity. Women were in a special category—placed on a pedestal and endowed with special virtues (again by European standards) but denied political and economic status. But inequality was likewise rooted in white male society, as was noted in a previous chapter. "Old families"—descendants of colonial (WASP) fortunes—viewed themselves as the conservators of those qualities which Tocqueville had identified as endangered by democracy: elevation of the mind, a scorn of mere temporal advantages, embellishment of manners, cultivation of the arts, promotion of love of beauty, and of glory.[11] Class-consciousness begat exclusiveness—the organization of an elite society to which newly-acquired wealth could not purchase admission. E. Digby Baltzell, perhaps the outstanding analyst of this class and its social role, comments: "Living near one another, on the gentle slope of Murray Hill in New York, on Beacon Street in Boston, or around Rittenhouse Square in Philadelphia, the members of these families knew who belonged within this formal and well-structured world of polite society."[12] Theodore Roosevelt, when a student at Harvard (graduating in 1880), could write to his sister that while he ranked nineteenth in a class of 230, "only one gentleman stands ahead of me."[13]

A second stratum of privilege developed alongside the old aristocracy and burgeoned after the Civil War—the new plutocracy, on whom the social elite looked down. In its early manifestation in the first half of the nineteenth century, these "self-made" men seemed to represent all that the old aristocracy opposed and hence were identified as champions of democracy. But as the century wore on, the new fortunes acquired powers of their own which seemed to become entrenched (riches did not dissolve into rags) and to be used to prevent the advance of others who aspired to wealth. Members of this new upper class, preoccupied above all else with the economic base of their position, were as exclusivist in that regard as the older elite was in its aristocratic pretensions. The exclusion took a different form—monopoly positions which repulsed would-be invaders—but it was exclusion nonetheless.

These two upper-class strata—the old aristocracy and the new plutocracy—in time combined to protect their privileged positions. Uneasy allies, they found common cause in combating populist efforts at redistribution, most notably in opposing a tax on incomes. Nevertheless, in a country dedicated to popular government and political equality, their defense could not be purely a negative one. Some concessions were necessary. The Interstate Commerce Act of 1887 was hailed as a major step in preventing the railroad magnates abusive use of power against small shippers. The Sherman Anti-Trust Act of 1890 would curb the efforts of big business to exclude competitors. But such concessions had their main impact in helping to preserve a general belief in prevailing social values—focal, constitutional, and distributive.

With the organizational revolution in the twentieth century, two phenomena, which we noted previously, have their impact on the distributive ethic. The special position of the WASP aristocracy declines, and the sphere of competition is increasingly transferred from the economy at large to the large corporation. Since we have noted these two effects in another connection, we need not dwell long on them here.

William C. Bullitt, himself a Philadelphia gentleman, notes the class change through the words of the fictional hero of his novel *It's Not Done*. Writing to his expatriate brother, the hero comments on the changes which have taken place in Philadelphia ("Chesterbridge," in the novel):

The American Distributive Value

"The worst of it is that men who ought to be street cleaners and grocers and dry-goods clerks and butchers and mechanics, and would be in any other country, have millions and millions. They *are* the country to-day. We may have been here three hundred years and they may have been here twenty or fifty, but the whole taste of the country has become their taste and its standards have become their standards." [14]

The achievement-bent, new (moneyed) upper-class stream rises in importance. Slowly but increasingly after World War II, old family names are displaced by names of foreign (non-Anglo-Saxon) ancestry in the rosters of officers and executives of large corporations, law offices, and government agencies. Meritocracy, the new name of the old principle of competitive achievement under conditions of equal opportunity, receives greater stress, particularly as higher education (the key to the door of opportunity) is made more accessible to those without either social background or wealth. (Symbolically, the Pundits, an exclusive society organized at Yale in 1880, whose major annual affair was a champagne and lobster picnic in the spring on the green in front of the university library, disbanded in 1970 "when it was agreed that champagne and lobster would probably clash with the egalitarian sensibilities of Yale undergraduates.")[15]

Meritocracy as a distributive principle has the advantage of continuity with the past, stressing the personal rather than class basis for achievement. But linked as the concept has been to educational (more specifically, technical) preparation for institutional roles, it has aroused a considerable mass opposition which has found its intellectual spokesmen. This opposition centers on the "elitist" structure of higher education, with colleges and universities ranked by prestige, the prestigious institutions incapable of "assimilating" any large numbers who cannot pay their way or have had inadequate preparation. It also involves a belief that lack of specialized training is being unfairly used as a barrier to advancement of those without formal education.

The second effect—internalization within the large corporation of a more substantial segment of the competitive system—was signaled initially by the emergence of more serious labor-management controversies. It was not until the Industrial Conference convened by President Wilson after World War I, however, that business leaders generally were prepared to admit that the economic competition between worker and employer had become unbalanced. Even then they were unwilling to concede that independent labor unions were warranted to give greater equality in the labor bargain. Not until the years of the New Deal were unions given legal protection, and not until the rise of the CIO were the major corporations organized, allowing the terms of the wage bargain to be negotiated collectively. The distributive principle of competition was retained, but its individualistic character was modified in major sectors.

The impact of large-scale corporate activity on the distributive principle was further demonstrated during the Great Depression. With unemployment widespread and business activity at a distress level, there was relatively little economic performance about which to be competitive. Not only did this state of affairs affect the constitutional issue of laissez faire, as we noted in the preceding chapter, it likewise affected traditional concepts of what people had to do to earn their share of income. Under conditions of large-scale economic interdependence, individuals—and indeed, even corporations—might have the will to support themselves but be prevented by a general condition with which they could not by themselves cope. Thus the idea of social welfare took root, expanding after World War II. These programs did not supplant but supplemented the system of competitive distribution. They made provision for people in circumstances, such as unemployment and old age, in particular, where self-reliance could not be expected. Old age is not temporary, but unemployment should be, so that assistance to the unemployed can be conditional on readiness to work when the opportunity is offered. This has been the general concept of social welfare programs in the United States, at least until now—that they are supports, not substitutes, for a system which retains a basic belief in distribution by merit. The distributive value in the United States thus continues to stress competitive results under conditions of equal opportunity, however imperfect that equality may be. However, in order to retain that principle, economic concessions have been made to individuals who would have been considered "undeserving" in an earlier day.

Indeed, within a society tolerating very considerable discrepancies in wealth and income and refusing to justify those inequalities on any ground except the merit residing in the individual, the competitive principle *has* to play a more dominant role than in older societies where inherited privilege lingers on. Never mind that the rule has its exceptions as long as they are viewed as exceptions.

Small wonder that Europeans have always been struck by the intensity of American life. Offering material rewards as the purpose of individualistic competitive struggle which consumes the greater part of her people's energies, America has fused the focal, constitutional, and distributive values into an integrated social philosophy. Despite amendments to that philosophy over the years, Coolidge's shorter catechism remains the inspired word: the business of America is business.

III

CHALLENGES
TO CONTEMPORARY
VALUES

8

Challenges to the Focal Value

A NUMBER of changes in the objective circumstances of American society have raised challenges to its focal, constitutional, and distributive values. Without further modification, the familiar social values may prove less effective as the cement uniting diverse groups and peoples. Even with modification those values may no longer possess their old magic. In this and the following two chapters we shall explore the major issues which are being raised. In doing so, it is well to keep in mind that any challenge to America's values is necessarily also a challenge to its business leaders, since the institution, which they represent, more than any other single influence, has shaped the challenged values.

The focal value of material accumulation for purposes of increased consumption (dignified, in a phrase worthy of Emerson, as "a rising standard of living") has been called into question on the dual grounds of whether it should be pursued and whether it can be sustained. These challenges have been so well publicized that there is no need to discuss them at length. It will be enough to summarize the arguments. The central thesis is that the world in general is fast approaching the point where further economic development will either not be possible or will be possible only under conditions that make it undesirable. Such a state of affairs clearly challenges the conception of material advancement as the chief social objective.

The reasons for this bleak prediction can be stated succinctly:

The *demand* for consumer goods has been rising astronomically, due to expanding world population (doubling every 35 years or so) and to rising incomes. (And rising incomes are not limited to the already affluent West; developing nations have also been adding to their per capita incomes.)

The *supply* of consumer goods will be unable to keep pace with rising demand, due to physical exhaustion of certain natural resources (especially fossil fuels and minerals) and the necessity of curbing industrial growth because of its polluting effects on the environment. (Pollution not only adversely affects water and air, it also changes atmospheric temperature.)

Even when raw materials are not exhausted, it will be necessary to resort to lower grades or less accessible sources, increasing costs of production. And if pollution effects can be controlled, it can only be done at added expense. The increase in supply costs will make the struggle for a rising standard of living self-defeating. In order to expand output, prices will have to rise, leading less to an increase in production than to a *shift* in production to supply the demands of the wealthy. Since this effect would be politically unacceptable to the much larger number of low-income receivers, both domestically and internationally, it would exacerbate the present political instability.

Further, the search for new resources for additional production ultimately exploits areas (localities, regions, countries) in ways which, while economically advantageous, involve less desirable modes of living. The locality chosen as the site for a nuclear power plant feels that it is being sacrificed so that *other* people's consumption can continue to rise. The rich farmlands of the West and Middle West are dug up to reach the coal beneath them, leading the editors of the *Atlantic* to ask, "Shall we strip-mine Iowa and Illinois to air-condition New York?" [1] The less-industrialized but resource-rich countries resent being drained of their natural wealth in the name of a free-trade system that is not of their own devising and does not provide them any greater sense of self-development or independence. In all these cases resource exploitation induces a sense of social exploitation, again undermining political equilibrium.

These warnings that there are limits to economic growth which, if exceeded, can only invite social conflict and deterioration of the quality of human life have been vigorously contested. The counterarguments are as familiar as the arguments themselves and need only be mentioned.

On the demand side, it is argued that the "demographic transition"—the historically demonstrated decline of family size with the rise of family affluence—will in time curb the pressure of population on resources. The faster the pace of economic development, the sooner that transition will be made. Moreover, if resources become scarcer, or if expanded industrial production requires unacceptable levels of pollution, society will re-order its priorities (more services instead of goods, for example), or will accept a somewhat slower rate of economic growth, or will channel more of its resources into improved methods of production. To insure pollution abatement, government, if necessary, can impose "effluent charges," a form of taxation which makes more costly those products or methods of production whose use should be curbed. With any or all of these effects occurring, there is no need for growth to grind to a halt. Further, the politically destabilizing effects of growth, both domestically and internationally, can be dealt with by such social devices as manpower training, technical assistance, and income redistribution from the wealthy to the poor.

On the supply side, history has conclusively demonstrated that resources are simply uncertain rather than definably finite. New deposits of resources are always being discovered, and new knowledge is always revealing the economic value of materials previously regarded as useless. The fear of running out of resources is unrealistic given the vast unexplored earth mass and ocean depths. If some particular natural product, like petroleum, should indeed become scarcer, conservation in its use would automatically be assured by its rising price, and at the same time its higher cost would effectively spur the search for substitutes. Moreover, continuing advances in technology guarantee that improved methods of production will be forthcoming, using scarce resources more efficiently and with less pollution. Indeed, in technology as in the production of other goods, increased demand leads to increased supply: the need for particular technical solutions will induce technicians to concentrate on those problems. Can anyone doubt, for example, that energy shortages will be met, soon enough, by harnessing the sun, the wind, the tides—all pollution free? Expanded production, in fact, makes possible the earlier development of more sophisticated technology: growth sustains itself.

There are several "clinching" counterarguments if the above are not accepted. It would be pointless for any one society to attempt to limit its economic growth, since other societies could be expected to take advantage of such self-denial by pressing ahead more vigorously. A society which deliberately abstained from economic growth would simply make itself more vulnerable to others which expanded. Finally, the alternatives to a higher standard of living through economic expansion are themselves unacceptably destabilizing. Institutions would have to be redesigned (what would motivate a business corporation if it were told it could not seek to expand its sales?). Income and wealth would have to be redistributed through government programs to satisfy the demands of those who feel discriminated against and who would use their numbers, democratically, to insist on relief. This could only be accomplished through government regulation, which would necessitate a more authoritarian society, endangering individual liberties.

Opposition to programs which would limit consumption or make it more costly does not emanate solely from the business sector, which is most directly involved. The very fact that consumption has become a value, the *focal* value, in American society means that most people, even if in varying degree, have come to accept and are willing to defend a rising standard of living, in the material sense, as the objective which most rules their lives. People's jobs and incomes depend on continuously increasing consumption: labor unions join with managements in decrying any restraints on output and in petitioning for government stimulants to consumption in times of unemployment.

Nevertheless, the contemporary challenge to the prevailing social objective has not been silenced. The debate goes on. Each of the counter-arguments can be met by surrebuttal. The hypothesis of the demographic transition is based on the experience of societies starting at lower rates of population growth and higher levels of economic advancement, with supporting social values already firmly implanted, in institutions as well as individuals. The reliance on technology is self-defeating, as the new developments generate their own problems, not always foreseen, or entail risks to human survival (nuclear radiation, depletion of the ozone layer, just for starters) not worth the trivial additions to consumption which they make possible.

At bottom, the debate reduces to two contending propositions. On the one hand, the adverse effects of continued economic growth are ultimately inescapable, even if postponable for a time by sheer luck and a variety of makeshift devices—we should, then, anticipate and change our ways. On the other hand, we can only guess at the future—we may as well make optimistic guesses as pessimistic ones, and so continue on our merry way.

But the way, for some, is no longer so merry. Preoccupation with consumption as a way of life has excluded other objectives. Foremost among these is the satisfaction to be derived from meaningful work well done.

Attitudes toward work have varied widely. In slave-owning societies physical labor has generally been viewed as demeaning. The Genesis story could be interpreted in a way that pictured a world free of work as Paradise, and the need to work for a living (the sweat of labor, to win one's bread) as a curse which mankind had brought on itself. However, in Catholic countries from the Middle Ages to the present century, the skill of the artisan was highly regarded; the greatest of artists were considered simply as superior artisans. To the artisan, the satisfaction derived from completion of a good piece of work (the fashioning of a pot, a doorframe, a pair of shoes, a piece of jewelry) was, no less than the money received for the product, part of the reward for labor. Granted that the work would not have been undertaken if it did not bring a price; it was almost as true that it would not have been undertaken if it did not bring some pleasure in the doing. For unskilled workers there was no such psychic reward, to be sure, but apprenticeship, formal or otherwise, was a readily available means of acquiring a skill.

In Protestant European countries, and in America, such an attitude held over from earlier days, for a time. But the Calvinist-Puritan emphasis was more upon labor as a duty, on one's vocation as the discharge of an obligation to God and fellow-men. The pleasing of self in the process was if anything a sign of waywardness, a temptation to be overcome. Bentham embodied the sterner attitude toward labor in his utilitarian philosophy when he identified work as pain, though in making it justifiable primarily by the pleasure of the consumption which it purchased he was ahead of his time—but not by much. For, at the time that Bentham wrote, Eli Whitney was busily developing, in the United States, the principles of mass production, not only the division of labor of Adam Smith's pin factory, but also standardization and the use of interchangeable parts. With the perfection and expansion of mass production came exactly the trade-off which Bentham had built into his felicific calculus—so much labor (pain) exchanged for so much consumption (pleasure), with satisfaction from doing the job not entering into the bargain at all.

Indeed, the very idea of "job" changed content. A job was no longer a specific undertaking, begun and completed, with another job to follow, but what one did day after day, with little or no variation, as part of a process, often (usually) meaningless by itself. Henry Ford hypnotized the world by the starkness with which he dramatized this modern interpretation of work and the job. The individual's role in production was reduced to the lowest common denominator of so many arm motions a minute; his pay was raised to the then fantastic level of five dollars a day; the price of the consumption goods he bought with his pay was lowered by the economies of the mass production of which he was part. (Automobiles available for the common man—a Ford for $600.)

Productivity was the key, and in the years that followed improved productivity became a principal objective of national economic policy, the means for achieving higher levels of per capita GNP. Productivity could arise from more effective capital equipment, from improved sources of raw material, from superior management, and from a variety of factors other than the contribution of workers. However, the labor factor (cost per unit of output) was important, and rising productivity was generally accompanied by greater specialization, less room for the human element, more tending of machines and equipment. Machine-tending might require considerable expertise, specialized, to be sure, but the relation between machines and men is quite different from the relation between men and tools. Control over the process is no longer with the worker.

Even for managers, without machine pacing, work has lost the satisfaction that comes from doing. As corporations have diversified and expanded their markets, each manager becomes less involved with and less concerned about the product for which he is in some degree responsible. What counts is his contribution to corporate profit performance and whether he "makes budget." If that involves sacrificing a little quality (but not sales, the quality loss must not show) or encouraging a throw-away attitude on the part of buyers ("end, not mend"), that is part of the job. One should not become emotionally involved with the product when the objective is rational calculation of how to make more money for the company and oneself. David Finn, of the public relations firm Ruder and Finn, who has dealt with many a corporate executive, muses: "Consciously he may think he loves his business and will do anything he can for it. Unconsciously he may hate it, resent the great burdens it places on his personal life, yearn to free himself of the slavery of his job. . . . Consciously he may believe that the need to satisfy the financial demands made by his family justifies his personally unrewarding labors. Unconsciously he may know that such demands are imaginary and that his family's greatest wish is that he free himself from the obsessive relationship he has with his company." [2]

Regarding both rank-and-file workers and managers by any objective standards, one might feel compelled to agree with the late literary critic, Edmund Wilson, when he declared, in the despair of the Great Depression, "The Buicks and Cadillacs, the bad gin and Scotch, the radio concerts interrupted by advertising talks, the golf and bridge of the suburban household, which the bond salesman can get for his money, can hardly compensate him for daily work of a kind in which it is utterly impossible to imagine a normal human being taking satisfaction or pride—and the bond salesman is the type of the whole urban office class." [3] To the white-collar class of Wilson's special concern many people would add blue-collar workers with their fragmented, specialized, and trivialized tasks.

Workers' dissatisfaction with the job as activity has become quite commonplace, as surveys have repeatedly showed, so commonplace that they tend to take it for granted, as a fact of life, to be accepted, perhaps improved a bit, but not basically altered. But surveys have also shown that workers tend to be relatively complacent about their jobs as a whole. Working conditions have improved, relations between men and managers are more equitable, thanks largely to unions, and above all the pay is good. Good wages have provided a steadily rising standard of living, a cornucopia of new gadgets and a well-filled larder. If the job provides little satisfaction, the pay-off does. Maybe work can be made less demanding, but who expects it to be fun? Despite a rather prevalent feeling that it would be nice if jobs provided more interest, this represents for most workers a dreamy wish rather than a call to radical reform. They are unprepared to scale down their immediate goods-wants to accommodate ephemeral job-wants.

Suppose, however, we treat job dissatisfaction not by itself as a threat to the present focal value but as such in company with other values which are also excluded by the overriding preoccupation with material advancement. A number of thoughtful individuals have de-cried the use of consumer goods as substitutes for emotions and ac-tivities, as a form of drugs on which a people become mindlessly hooked. An adventure with nature turns into an assembly of camp-ers' gadgets stowed in a camping trailer; enjoyment of swimming comes with a private swimming pool; education is something to be purchased at an institution equipped with the latest facilities. But if, ultimately, there are some wants which cannot be satisfied through material channels, whose satisfaction may in fact be frustrated by a materialist orientation, and such wants tend to cumulate *as a direct consequence of economic growth,* then conceivably frustrations may mount to the point where the consumption ethic faces a serious challenge.

Gregory Bateson is one who worries that our contemporary soci-ety has so fixed itself on the pursuit of "selective purpose," such as economic growth, that we have lost the sense of balance, or what he calls "systemic wisdom." [4] We focus on an objective without re-spect to the impact on the rest of the social and natural system. Be-havior is specialized to achieve certain results at the expense of others. Science serves up a bag of tricks to be put at the use of the specialized purpose. "Planning," whether of big corporations or of governments, becomes constrained behavior in the pursuit of selec-tive objectives—planning *begins* with purpose. The terrible conse-quence of such selective purposive planning, says Bateson, is that, as in the case of any obsession, everything becomes sacrificed to it. When emergencies are confronted, they are solved by expediency. When other objectives (values) compete, they are ruthlessly overrid-den. The sense of balance is sacrificed to an irresponsible fixation.

It is such a fixation on material objectives which has led econo-mists and governments to argue that if we encounter shortages of some resources, we can simply substitute other resources or other technologies. If we suddenly become aware of air and water pollu-tion, this is because we have failed to consider air and water as eco-nomic goods. By treating them as goods to *buy,* by charging for them (for example, by cranking effluent charges into production costs or taxes), we can have as much of them as we want—want, that is to say, at their higher prices, in competition with other goods.

Suppose, however, it turns out that resources must be used with more of Bateson's systemic wisdom, because to do otherwise threatens the system. Suppose that "monkeying" with technological substitutes (nuclear energy) or convenience goods (ozone-affecting spray cans) upsets the life-sustaining "balance" of nature. Suppose the incontinent competitive pursuit by all of a "higher level" of consumption leads to domestic and international political disequilibrium. Conceivably there would be enough engendered dissatisfaction to dynamite even the most fixated belief in economic growth as the only solution to social problems, as the overriding social objective.

We thus come back to the present major challenge to the focal value of consumption. This is a belief that resources will not sustain such a social objective indefinitely and that to postpone recognition of that fact and to continue pursuing economic growth selectively and obsessively can lead only to the deterioration of civilization, not only subjectively but objectively—objective conditions which spell disaster. Loss in the emotional satisfaction of work—a job well done—may be one of the prices we have already paid for the materialist obsession, but it is by no means the most urgent or most important. Not only a way of life, but life itself may be at issue.

The substantiality of that prospect has already pursuaded some business leaders of the need for changed social behavior. Fletcher L. Byrom, Chairman of the Board of the Koppers Company, says: "There may be countering arguments, but I am willing to assume that, in terms of the needs of generations to come, many of the resources we now use and for which we have found no substitutes are in short supply and should be allocated to avoid waste. . . . We cannot continue to misuse our resources for life styles that are self-indulgent at their best and frivolous at their worst." [5] J. Edwin Matz, President of the John Hancock Mutual Life Insurance Company, writes: "Somehow one feels that ultimately there must be a better solution, that there needs to be a state of economic well-being which does not depend on an ever increasing number of people exploiting the finite resources of the planet at an ever accelerating rate." [6]

It is not likely to be any "sudden death" of civilization that we confront, if, on the one hand, we continue to grow, and if, on the other hand, we cannot continue to grow. But there is ample reason to expect that changing objective conditions—solid reality, which cannot be reasoned away—will make anachronistic and, in the end, self-defeating, institutionalized behavior based on organized competition for an ever larger slice of an ever-expanding pie.

There is no doubt that private competition in pursuit of material gain is a recipe for growth. But in making our social purpose so singular (and cumulative), bending all of nature to that one end, we threaten the natural conditions themselves, on which we depend, and there is not even a theoretical probability that we are wise enough—if powered by that compulsive motor—not to make good that threat, again and again.

9

=====

Challenges to the Constitutional Value

DESPITE major changes in the objective conditions of American society, individualism—individualism and the preference for private over government initiatives—has continued to be our creed. Despite the organizational revolution and the technological momentum, we maintain a primary concern for the impact of these on the individual. We wrestle with the problem of how to make the individual significant *in* the organization. If the organization seems on the point of overpowering the individual, we look for ways—including government regulation, as notably in the Wagner Act of 1935, the Landrum-Griffin Act of 1959, the Civil Rights Act of 1964—of bolstering the resistance power of the individual. If economic or social relations seem to have become so complex that *only* government can deal effectively with them, we more readily accept its intervention but still ask that it remove itself from the situation at the earliest opportunity.

This attitude, indeed, the conviction, is excellently illustrated in the gradual transformation of two major reformers and writers, Lincoln Steffens and John Dos Passos. Both moved from early flirtation with radical causes to ultimate affirmation that the American "way of life" was, if not best, better than available alternatives.

Steffens, prince of muckrakers, who once had been of the opinion that "only revolution could do the job," and who had inspected Russia after the revolution with critical sympathy, returned from his European wanderings at the end of the twenties with a new appreciation of "my amazing country." He recognized the dominant hold of business on America, but he had come to believe that business itself was imbued with "a new sense of democracy." [1] This was after World War I and before the Great Depression. Dos Passos, writing after the Depression and after World War II, makes the same transition, less naively. He too had seen Europe and Russia with initial sympathy but arrived at "the basic verity"—that "socialism is a new system of exploitation of man by man very much more total and without any of the loopholes that capitalism allows—through which the individual can escape and lead a life of comparative freedom and dignity." [2]

As a young man just out of college, Dos Passos had been embittered with the "great stupid mass of America . . . under the crushing weight of industry." "The idea of individual liberty does not exist any where." [3] Was it maturing wisdom or the complacency of middle years that had altered his vision? The answer is immaterial to the fact that even in his more optimistic later mood the *ideal* of individual liberty remained firm and freedom from governmental regulation and coercion were still to be fought for. It was only his appraisal of the possibilities of attaining "a life of comparative freedom and dignity" that had become rosier.

In the contemporary United States intellectual and reformist pilgrims are more likely to journey in a reverse direction from Steffens and Dos Passos, from a youthful height of optimism at the potential for sustaining individual freedoms to a depth of despondency in their maturity, at the unlikelihood of reaching that goal. Richard N. Goodwin provides a good example of this phenomenon. As a young man in his twenties, Goodwin began serving John Kennedy (and then Lyndon Johnson) as presidential counselor and speechwriter. Optimistically liberal in political outlook, he is credited with having written the "Great Society" and "War on Poverty" speeches of the

Johnson administration, advancing the position that American society could be stimulated to higher levels of "justice for all" under governmental initiative. By 1974, in *The American Condition,* his outlook had changed.[4] Optimism had given way to an almost determined pessimism, and governmental leadership could provide no exit from the slough of despond.

The philosophical basis for this forlorn conclusion was spread out over 400 pages. Any brief summary does violence to a fine-spun thesis, but the gist of Goodwin's argument is that the rise of *systems* thinking, embracing a total order and defining all of reality, has eroded the sense of an autonomous community. Community authority was usurped by more encompassing and impersonal authority, and in the process individual freedom, which can only be expressed within a meaningful social context, was undermined.

In the United States, the authority which systematically transcended self-control increasingly centered in technology (utilitarian science), and in technology's high priests, the corporate exploiters of technology. The years since World War II have only confirmed that locus of impersonal power.

If technology is the source of authority, then, according to Goodwin, bureaucracy is its logic. And since technology intrudes on most social relationships, its bureaucratic logic—expressed in the concepts and theory of systems analysis—embraces and smothers social relationships on the smaller, human scale where, only, they can be satisfying. Unresponsive and socially indifferent, large corporations are concerned only with their own survival and expansion. The tenders of these monstrous machines, a succession of temporary managers, are shaped to this end, and discarded if they abuse their temporary powers by using them for any significantly different purpose.

But Goodwin recognizes that the large corporation is not alone. It has generated the large labor and educational bureaucracies and the massive bureaucracies of the federal government—all integral to the system. Swollen in size, these are no longer as much controlled as controlling. All put distance between the individual and the authority at the top of the hierarchy. At one time corporations, labor unions, and universities, like government itself, were viewed as governed by their constituents through shareholder democracy, rank-and-file control, and faculty sovereignty. But with growth and size and complexity, the organization becomes first a system of its own, each part controlled by the overall design. Later, with growth and complexity continuing, it becomes a subsystem within a larger system, itself controlled by its prescribed relation to the rest of the system. Planning becomes inescapable in the face of complexity. Planning is a function of sovereignty. However, when the numbers involved become large, direct participation—indeed, even representation in any significant sense—in the exercise of sovereignty or planning is not feasible, either by all those composing a corporation, with respect to corporation planning, or by the population at large, in the case of public programs. Local plants, local unions, local governments feel manipulated by a distant "head office." In Marcuse's phrase "all domination assumes the form of administration." [5]

The consequence is a dehumanization of relationships, first within each bureaucracy and then through their combined influence within society as a whole. Like Marx, but without the class overtones, Goodwin expresses this dehumanization as alienation, the diminution of human life through man's subjection to his own creations. Out of their impotence to effect satisfying social relationships, people have been driven in on themselves, retreating into a trivialized individualism, devoid of significant social context. This is hardly the spontaneous individualism of Tocqueville's America which, along with private space, offered opportunities to join with others in effective political action, in community. Contemporary individualism—a withdrawal—only offers further opportunity for bureaucracy to expand.

The irony, or the tragedy, of the American condition of alienation and social fragmentation is that it arises from the *success* of the American system. Modern confusion and distress now reveal themselves, Goodwin emphasizes, as a consequence, not of human evil, but of the process which provides material abundance. We are not the victims of perfectable weakness in the social structure, he observes; rather, our humanity is being consumed *by the structure itself*. This is no Manichean conflict between the forces of evil and the forces of good contained within "one world"; it is as though God himself had been revealed as wicked.

Goodwin is not alone in his belief that America's failure lies in its success. Eric Hoffer, the proletarian philosopher, ruminates: "We are living in an epoch of great disillusionment. We are beginning to suspect that to fulfill a hope is to defeat it, and to make a dream come true is to turn it into a nightmare." [6] Robert Penn Warren expresses "the tragic ambiguity of the fact that the spirit of the nation we had promised to create has often been the victim of our astounding objective success, and that, in our success, we have put at pawn the very essence of the nation we had promised to create—that essence being the concept of the free man, the responsible self." [7]

Despite his appeal for a change in social values, the lament which Goodwin and others sing scarcely constitutes a challenge to the existing constitutional value of individualism. Even though now trivialized by bureaucratic operations, individualism is still perceived as a virtue. Even though business may be the principal purveyor of the bureaucratic blanket which covers individualism, the least that can be said in its defense is that there is greater freedom with dispersed private bureaucracies than under monolithic government bureaucracy, the principal realistic alternative. There is still freedom to be lost. In Dos Passos' modest assessment, the United States enjoys "comparative freedom."

The despair which characterizes Goodwin and a number of contemporary thinkers, and which briefly erupted on university campuses in 1968, can be viewed less as a challenge to the present constitutional value than as a loss of faith in its observance. The pessimism could be removed as easily by a recharging of the old belief as by an implanting of a new conviction. Even a skillful public relations campaign might do the trick.

A more genuine challenge to the constitutional value is posed by those who not only accept the existence of the technologic and bu-

Challenges to the Constitutional Value

reaucratic conditions whose effects Goodwin deplores, but see these as inescapably part of our objective conditions. To lament them is to surrender to romantic nostalgia. The future lies with those who adjust to them. In this view, to cling to an individualist philosophy under present circumstances is an act of social immaturity, comparable to the personal immaturity of an adult who refuses to shed his childish ways. The present forms and practices of both technologies and bureaucracies need not be taken as given, but can and should be used to improve the American condition.

A forceful expression of this view has come from Philip Hauser, past president of both the American Sociological Society and the National Conference of Social Welfare. A "social morphological revolution" has transformed the United States into a "metropolitan, industrialized mass society," in which insistence on individualism and self-determination represents an "anachronistic frontier psychology." He identifies as "outmoded slogans" and "shibboleths" such once-sacred tenets as:

— That government is best which governs least;
— Each man in pursuing his own interest . . . will be acting in the interest of the collectivity;
— We must adhere to our traditions of rugged individualism and free enterprise. . . .

While maintaining a belief in democratic principles, including representative government, Hauser urges that an "urban bill of rights" should provide for "an environment controlled in the interest of society, physical and social, free from pollution and adverse population densities and including adequate housing." To underscore the change in outlook from the American past, he restates the constitutional principle involved: "Especially significant is the provision to make the interests of society paramount over those of the individual—a provision that would in effect modify present provisions in the Constitution which place the right of the person above those of society." [8]

Hauser argues the necessity of social control because of radical

95

changes in the objective conditions, especially urbanization and the racial composition of urban populations. The psychologist B. F. Skinner goes further. While agreeing that changed conditions demand urgent solutions, he maintains that a developing science of behavior now permits the kinds of socially beneficent control over individuals which are necessary to cultural survival: "Autonomous man has reached a dead end." "A scientific analysis of behavior dispossesses autonomous man and turns the control he has been said to exert over to the environment," but an environment which society itself designs and constructs to make more effective the behavior of its members. [9]

The traditional constitutional value of personal autonomy appeals to ideas of "freedom" and "dignity." The individual is held responsible for his conduct and is said to merit whatever he achieves. Whatever advances the welfare of the individual is regarded by him as valuable, regardless of its social impact. Freedom is construed as the absence of constraint (*let* me—laissez faire). Dignity is acquired by a constant struggle *against* aversive controls, controls such as Goodwin ascribes to bureaucracies. But this is a myopic cause, Skinner asserts. It misses the fact that *all* human behavior is contingent on its *consequences*. To seek to remove only the painful, repressive consequences of behavior still leaves in place all the *positive* inducements to other forms of behavior.

In a society stressing individual freedom, the behavior induced is that which rewards the individual. In a society stressing its own survival, the behavior induced is that which benefits society. In both cases behavior is environmentally induced—neither is any freer than the other. Only the consequences differ. "Good government is as much a matter of the control of human behavior as bad," and approved incentives motivate people no less than the harsher forms of exploitation. If we reward private competitive behavior, we induce competitive behavior, at the expense of any obstacle in its way. But, if we reward cooperative behavior instead, then we will get cooperative behavior. "The technology of behavior which emerges is ethically neutral, but when applied to the design of a culture, the survival of the culture functions as a value." [10]

If America continues to make individual freedom and autonomy its principal constitutional value, sooner or later it will have to give way to another society which puts its cultural survival first, and engineers its institutions to reinforce, by reward, the kind of behavior which contributes to that end. "The intentional design of a culture and the control of human behavior it implies are essential if the human species is to continue to develop." And this objective is impeded—threatened—by "the literatures of freedom and dignity." [11]

With Skinner, it is not technology or bureaucracy which has jeopardized the American condition, but the failure to use these appropriately as instruments for rewarding socially desirable behavior. It is the cult of individualism which constitutes the chief threat to society. There is a dichotomous choice between science or disaster. "When a science of behavior has once been achieved, there's no alternative to a planned society. We can't leave mankind to an accidental and biased control." [12]

For the philosopher Isaiah Berlin there is a different forced choice, though ultimately it appears to confront the same major issues of Skinner's dichotomy. Science is not involved, only people's aspirations, their values. His argument is laid out in a penetrating analysis of Machiavelli's political opinions, in which he seems to accept, for himself, the validity—"this painful truth"—of the thesis he ascribes to Machiavelli. [13]

Western society has tended to emphasize the primacy of individual morality, a principle engendered by its Greco-Hebraic-Christian background. (We note here that the Protestant Reformation strengthened that individualistic assertion, and that nowhere did the Reformers have so pervasive an influence as in the United States.) Since people are by nature social and political, individualism cannot be construed as a denial of community, nor can individual morality be considered something opposed to politics. On the contrary, individualism constitutes one *form* of political organization and morality. There is, however, an alternative form, a competing political organization with its own ethic—public greatness, the great society—the Athens of Pericles and the Rome of Augustus Caesar are famous examples. A people must choose one or the other, it cannot have both. If it chooses individualism, it gives up hope of becoming an Athens or Rome. If it opts for the great society, its members then must subordinate their consciences and interests to the power and glory of the state. (Moreover, by assuming *public* office an individual must abandon private morality as a guide, something of special interest to Machiavelli but of less interest to us.)

In quiet times the two contending political moralities may indeed survive, haphazardly, alongside each other. The American space program, for example, was not so much evidence of a democratic society's capability for national greatness as a demonstration of its willingness to suspend or dilute, in a fit of pique, its affirmed values of private enterprise directed to individualistic objectives. It was a public program instituted by presidential—almost imperial—edict, as a direct response to the Russian challenge, aimed to go the Russians one better by taking the moon. The program was a highly centralized undertaking, given priority over other (private) objectives— a kind of extended military-science campaign in space. But if this misalliance of two distinctive political forms—an attempted coupling of national greatness and individualism—is subjected to conditions of continuing stress their antinomy stands revealed. In Berlin's words, ''One is obliged to choose: and in choosing one form of life, give up the other.''

The preference for individualism, however secularized in modern times, still carries the mark of its religious inspiration, opposing personal conscience to social artifice. In doing so, it ignores the possibility that such a society, founded on the autonomous individual, may be too disjointed, too loosely hung together, to survive. However much ''one may prefer a state in which citizens are prosperous even though the public treasury is poor, in which government is neither centralized nor omnipotent, nor, perhaps, sovereign at all, but the citizens enjoy a wide degree of individual freedom,'' for Machiavelli (here Berlin does not say whether he endorses this view) such a state cannot last. When a society has lost its appetite for greatness, it is doomed to decadence and eventual plucking by more vigorous and purposeful states.

The American constitutional value, however amended and reinterpreted, is rooted in the assumption that no choice between individualism and a great state need be made, that one, indeed, assures the other. The "Great Society" program launched by President Johnson was justified as necessary to make individualism work for everybody. But such emphasis on the person, particularly in a society where a substantial minority feels exploited, can lead to preoccupation with the removal of what Skinner calls the aversive controls—constraints on individual behavior. This preoccupation and the underlying disunity of American society subvert any efforts at dignifying the social *entity,* which is viewed as a specious abstraction.

It is not from dissatisfaction with the oppressiveness of institutions that one can discern the gravest challenge to the existing constitutional value. That kind of dissatisfaction stems precisely from continued *acceptance* of the traditional value. The challenge comes, rather, from those who, for whatever reason, believe that individualism, even when supplemented by the concerns of a welfare state, is inadequate to cope with existing conditions. Hauser comes to this conviction because of the march of events—the facts of institutional, cultural, historical change and the necessity of dealing with them empirically, pragmatically, justicially. Skinner believes we can now, and should, opt for social control over the individual because the advance in scientific knowledge makes that solution feasible and rational, and because that solution is necessary for our survival as a society. Berlin suggests that an ethical choice must be made between two incompatible goals—the free individual in a disorganized society, or the great society in which the individual finds his fulfillment. All three positions, though differing in significant details, are compatible with each other on the major issue. They are cumulative in their influence as direct challenges to America's present constitutional value. In contrast to those who only lament a lost individualism, the idea of social leadership provides a vision of a different America.

The idea sounds dangerous. Distorted, the vision may prove a nightmare. But what if circumstances are pushing us—as Hauser and Skinner believe—toward a state where the alternative is disaster?

10

Challenges to the
Distributive Value

T HE PRINCIPLE on which American society has traditionally sought to distribute its benefits has been competition within a framework of equal opportunity. Social status earned by birth—the aristocratic principle—has had a hard time surviving, and since World War II is all but dead. Differential economic rewards are still influenced by inheritance, but the effects of inherited advantage have been eroded by a variety of governmental programs aimed at improving the competence of individuals to compete.

This principle of rewarding people according to their achievements retains widespread support. A survey conducted by a Harvard group under Professor Lee Rainwater led to the conclusion that "Few of our respondents regard a well-functioning meritocracy as a bad idea." People believed in the principles of equal opportunity and equal treatment for all, recognized that the present system functioned imperfectly and could be improved, but thought that even with its blemishes it was, basically, not exploitative.[1]

The apparent consensus on this principle, however, has been proving to be more and more illusory. Since the early 1960s—coincident with but not necessarily triggered off by the federal government's

"War on Poverty"—the idea has been gaining ground that unequal conditions breed unequal opportunity. If equal opportunity is the empirical basis on which meritocracy can be justified as the chief distributive principle, then more must be done to equalize conditions.

The idea was not wholly new to the United States; what *was* new was its sweep. There had been scattered pressures for redistribution in every depression in the nineteenth century. There had been little support, however, even from low-income groups, for the idea that people were entitled to payment out of the public treasury simply because they were poor. That some persons robbed the public, that such malefactors should be deprived of their special privileges, that exploiters should be clipped of their power to exploit—all that, yes; people could then provide for themselves under more equitable conditions. And it was admitted also that there were some in hardship, through no fault of their own, whose needs were greater than their capacity to provide. These—the "deserving poor"—would be taken care of by voluntary charity, either by their neighbors or by wealthy philanthropists.

Even in the Great Depression, New Deal legislation aimed not so much at redistribution as at leveling up (minimum wage laws and protection for labor organizations) and providing social insurance (for old age, for unemployment) to be bought by workers or employers or both, and supplemented by public subsidy. Direct relief was regarded as a purely temporary palliative to "prime the pump," to get the system going again so that such relief would no longer be needed.

The "pump" never did get primed. Only the artificial prosperity of World War II ended the spectacle of large-scale poverty due to lack of jobs. On the premise that jobs were the remedy for low incomes, supplemented by social insurance for those unable to work, the immediate postwar period emphasized the need for full employment, a state of the economy to be insured by government fiscal and monetary measures. This was the "new economics," the gospel according to Keynes. However theoretically valid, it failed to take into account two political phenomena. First, following the Ricardian principle of employing marginal resources last, business firms, in hiring, excluded the least wanted types of workers—racial and certain ethnic minorities, women, the poorly educated (except for certain kinds of common labor), and misfits and deviants. There had always been people in these categories but there had been little feeling of social responsibility for them. Now their numbers, in absolute terms, were larger, and they were more concentrated in the major cities. To absorb these people into the ranks of the employed required stimulation of the economy to inflationary levels—overheating it, in the phrase widely used. Moreover, many were not covered by social insurance, since that required a work nexus, which was precisely what they lacked.

Second, for reasons not susceptible to definite explanation, a new wave of egalitarianism was sweeping the world, and the United States was not immune to its effects. World War II was probably a factor, unleashing sentiments of anti-colonialism, anti-capitalism, and anti-white-westernism. Perhaps it was simply the latest stage in Tocqueville's seven-centuries-long egalitarian movement, or in Ortega y Gassett's revolt of the masses. Conceivably, it was pushed along by academic theorists imbued with the egalitarian philosophy and unable to rationalize existing distributive differentials by any acceptable principle. In any event, numbers of those in the ranks of the unemployed refused to accept jobs considered demeaning and servile, and their refusal was widely approved by egalitarian sentiments. The pressure of low income or unemployment was insufficient to force their acceptance of such casual, poorly paid, and menial jobs as might be available—the kind of jobs that had provided, however inadequately, for people in their circumstances in earlier years. They became, especially in urban concentrations, contributors to the statistics of the unemployed—statistics which themselves are a modern phenomenon, whose very existence creates a pressure on government to "do something" about the situation statistically revealed.

It was not that the numbers of the poor had increased in the years since World War II. By any definition of poverty (except the one that defines it as the lowest one-fifth or one-third or some other in-variant percentage of the population), their numbers had declined startlingly.[2] But those who were in this category were more visible and more vocal. The mass movement of blacks from the South to Northern, Central, and Western cities, joined by large numbers from the Caribbean islands and Mexico, pushed more affluent whites into the suburbs, leaving the metropolitan areas peaks of poverty and half nonwhite. This compactness of location coincided, perhaps not ac-cidentally, with a new sense of cohesion among the nonwhites, who, while minorities in the nation, were rapidly becoming majorities in the major cities. It also coincided with a surging civil rights move-ment under a new and vigorous leadership and with a radical rejec-tion of the authority system which they found oppressive.

Following a wave of black violence in city after city in the sum-mers of 1967 and 1968, the anti-poverty programs which had issued from the Johnson administration in 1964 were supplemented by pri-vate, voluntaristic, largely business-supported programs aimed at opening up more jobs for the so-called ''hard-core unemployed'' and training them (in social as well as vocational skills) to fill such jobs. The Urban Coalition and National Alliance of Businessmen were two of the most prominent organizations sponsoring such programs. In the cities themselves there was a massive increase in welfare loads to ease the sting of poverty and alienation, an expansion of municipal payrolls, with a rising proportion of the new population manning programs intended to be responsive to their own needs. In effect, the business and middle-class populations were allied in granting con-cessions to a protesting and disruptive minority in order to keep peace in the system as a whole.

But the system could not so easily be patched or restored. Once a compact minority (with some degree of organization) has latched onto the idea that it wields political power, the possibility emerges for a serious and continuing confrontation. This happened, in the United States, at first within the cities themselves, and then between all cities with minority concentrations and the rest of society. The militancy of the racial minorities does not spring from the desperation of those who have nothing to lose. Indeed, dependent as so many are on public largesse, they have a great deal to lose. It is the impermanence of their economic position which induces the more aggressive to demand that society accept them by vesting their benefits as rights—the "new property," in Charles Reich's phrase—and by augmenting those incomes to a level more closely approximating others' incomes. To *demand* public benefits as *rights* rather than charity lends greater dignity to the recipients.

The concept of equality which requires society, as a matter of justice, to offset with remedial programs personal inadequacies which are no fault of the individual, has gained a liberal intellectual following. The Harvard philosopher John Rawls made a considerable stir in intellectual circles with the publication in 1971 of *A Theory of Justice* in which he espoused the principle that since the adverse inequalities stemming from family and natural endowment are "undeserved"—acts of Nature, as it were—these should somehow be compensated for by people who were more benefited by equally fortuitous circumstance. In order to achieve the ideal of treating all people equally, and thus providing genuine equality of opportunity, society must shift resources to those born with fewer native assets or a less favorable social position.

In a similar vein, if less philosophically, a member of the University of Wisconsin's Center for Poverty Research was quoted as saying that when the federal Office of Economic Opportunity was created in 1964, its architects were excessively optimistic about the beneficial effects of job training and additional education. "Back then we thought that giving people equal opportunity was a big step. But we found"—this was in 1974—"that even with equal opportunity, some people still don't have equal opportunity to take advantage of equal opportunity. People must have incomes, that's the answer." [3]

However influential such philosophical social-science arguments are, a more commonsense attitude seemed to be that if equality of opportunity were functioning properly there would be fewer people in poverty than is actually the case. Rainwater found, in his Boston sample, "a kind of ambivalent readiness for redistribution if it can be done in a way that does not deny the validity of merit, effort, and achievement as the basis for rewards in society." [4]

This egalitarian sentiment made the War on Poverty good politics and led to an explosive expansion of welfare expenditures on the part of governments at all levels. Federal spending on social programs increased 6½ times in fifteen years, from approximately $21 billion in 1960 to $131 billion in 1975. Medicaid and Medicare, which did not even exist in the earlier year, by 1975 were disbursing some $20 billion. Medical care had come to be viewed as a right which society owed to its citizens. A food-stamp program, inaugurated in 1964 "to alleviate hunger and malnutrition," in 1975 was serving over 14 million people at a cost of close to $4 billion. So fast was the rate of increase in this one program that Congress, which in 1971 had passed a law requiring states to publicize its availability, became anxious enough to explore limits on its further expansion. Despite Congressional perturbation, exponents of equalization have seen in food stamps a model for other forms of assistance. Food stamps, which are purchased at a discount by those whose income and needs qualify them, could be followed by housing allowances, then clothing coupons—where need the line be drawn? Tocqueville's admonition of the previous century comes hauntingly to mind: whenever the poor dominate politics, they inflate public expenditures.

At the same time that federal expenditures on social welfare programs were rising at a rapid rate, additional amounts were being contributed by states and local communities (in fiscal 1976, the state of California was expected to contribute $2 billion, the city of New York somewhat more than that), and were likewise subject to escalation (New York City's spending increased five times in the ten years beginning 1964). Considerable controversy centered on two issues— whether assistance was going to families which included an employable member, and whether the lists contained an excessive proportion of ineligibles. (Among numerous studies, one in New York City found that in May 1974 half the welfare and relief cases had a member capable of work, and another that in the first four months of

1975 of those receiving welfare 9% were ineligible. Other studies of different periods have found different results, some higher, some lower.) Nevertheless, the egalitarian sentiment has been strong enough to mute the criticism implicit in the issues raised. When the mayor of Newburgh, New York sought to require able-bodied recipients of public assistance to render some public service in return, he was so vigorously condemned that he withdrew the requirement. Compulsory work as a prerequisite to survival was viewed as taking advantage of those in an unfortunate (unequal) state.

Such is the hold of social values that once inculcated they may induce sentiments which, in any crude material sense, run counter to self-interest. Indeed, that is one of their functions; Marx inveighed against them for that reason. Thus the egalitarian principle can lead to redistributive policies which those who approve, in theory, fight in reality when the incidence falls on them. Thus, most middle-class and working people in Rainwater's Boston sample believed that lower incomes should be leveled up, though many from that same strata have been among the most vocal in protesting the taxes and welfare programs which make that possible.

But there is more to the matter than simply an instinctive response to appeals invoking long-respected values. There is a disconnectedness between government revenue-spending for welfare programs and government revenue-raising to support those programs, so that the individual citizen can establish no direct relation between them. Does he believe in food-stamps for hungry people? Of course. How much will they cost the government? He has no idea. Perhaps nothing—maybe the food has already been acquired under farm-subsidy programs previously or presently paid for. Even if not, would he be willing to contribute? To be sure—how much can it be? Perhaps something akin to a small charitable contribution. What? Four billion dollars? But after all, that is a small sum compared to the $265 billion dollars or so the government is spending. How much of it comes out of his pocket? How can he tell—it would depend on the amount of his taxes relative to what other people are paying. An inflationary effect? Who's to say—not even the economists. In the light of all that uncertainty, why fight what looks like a decent thing to do?

At the same time put into the picture the role of the professional politicians, the brokers of power, those who must mediate between contending interests. The pressures for assistance or remedial action emanating from those who experience need or feel inequitably treated come to rest on the political representatives. The more compact, the more organized those pressures, the more they must be listened to. Votes are behind those pressures and can be swung to other politicians if there is an unsympathetic response. Moreover, the professional politician, no less than the average citizen, makes no direct connection between expenditures for a program and the means of financing them. Where will the money come from? Why, "the budget," of course. What if "the budget" will not accommodate all expenditures? That's for the Management and Budget Office to worry about—a little tinkering here, a little there, some borrowing if need be. Indeed, the legislator does not want to make a connection; Congress is only now experimenting with procedures for unmasking the budgetary impact of its legislation, and still is reluctant to comply with its recently self-imposed requirement that all expenditures which it approves be accommodated within a fixed limit, which would oblige it to make difficult choices. Its preference is to honor popular pressures for disbursements (somebody's "due," some group's "equity," some compensation for those whose opportunities are not "equal") without worrying, at the time, about the payments problem.

One of the effects of these several egalitarian pressures is to create an inflationary impetus. If jobs must be provided for all, or nearly all—"full employment," however that may be defined—and especially if this includes numbers of individuals poorly equipped for employment, then fiscal policy (taxing and spending) and monetary policy (credit availability, both private and public) must be geared to create high-employment conditions. If those who cannot be swept into paying jobs by such gross measures must nevertheless be supplied with incomes which entitle them to a standard of living not too far down the scale to be embarrassing and potentially incendiary, then welfare programs must be expanded and financed even if by public borrowing.

The wage-earners who are marginally hired under full-employment programs make only a marginal contribution to output—that much of the economist's marginal-productivity theory of wages is valid. The recipients of public assistance make no contribution at all. The effect is to increase the number of claimants proportionate to the total output. Prices go up. If some components of total output do increase proportionately, due to rising productivity or the availability of unused capacity, then perhaps (though not certainly) only prices of the less flexible components will increase. Or if additional capacity exists but can turn out additional goods only with some delay, then prices may go up only "temporarily," however long that may be. In any event the general price level will rise. The efforts to create a demand high enough to require the services of those least easily assimilated into the labor force, and to accommodate the now much larger number of those eligible for public assistance, guarantee that.

The inflationary consequences of full employment and welfare programs could be largely dispelled if people with above-average incomes would *consent* to subsidize those with below-average incomes, that is, if an actual transfer of income took place between those most responsible for the system's functioning and those least responsible. Inflation—secular inflation—could be avoided in an earlier day because society's less fortunate members by and large accepted their misfortune, and were content with such assistance as was voluntarily channeled to them. But when they demand more, and mobilize their political strength more effectively to secure it, the concessions made are no longer voluntary (as private charity had been earlier). More accurately, the concessions made are retracted by an unwillingness to back them with an adequate transfer of income. By a variety of devices, not always with explicit intention, upper-income receivers hold on to their advantage while seeming to reduce it. Some transfer does of course take place, but not enough to prevent inflationary pressures as people with redistributed income try to spend what has not, in fact, been redistributed. The disconnection between governmental spending and governmental receipts makes this state of affairs possible without exposing its mechanism, without, indeed, anyone's having cause to feel guilty about the consequences. In the words of Treasury Secretary William Simon, "We begin with the best of intentions," but then things spin out of control. Simon was referring to the escalation of the food-stamp program, and its exploitation by "chiselers and rip-off artists," but his phrase, "best intentions," has more poignant overtones than he was aware.[5] "Best intentions" underly all social programs, but have only paved a road to an inflationary hell because the intentions have not been validated by actual transfers of income. What is at fault? Is the good intention misguided, or is the failed performance the real sin?

The question of who is responsible for inflation is akin to the question of who is responsible for a labor strike. Is it the workers and their unions who make demands, or the employers who refuse those demands? Of course a strike would not occur if workers were compliant and content; equally, no strike would occur if employers were generous and yielding. Are the demands "too high"? By whose standards?

Inflation would not occur (the language is too strong; other factors are also involved, but the point is more easily made by concentrating on only this one influence) if upper-income groups consented to have enough of their income redistributed to low-income receivers in response to egalitarian pressures. Are egalitarian demanders or privileged resisters responsible for the resulting inflation? If income recipients at *all* levels then insist on being "compensated" for price effects, is this a matter of each seeking his "due," or should the more advantaged assent to the inflationary erosion of their incomes, without seeking compensatory increases, so that the less advantaged need not suffer so much?

Perhaps the most striking aspect of all discussions of economic justice is the lack of consideration of power, as though these two could be disentangled. But if social values are the reflection of the values of a dominant social stratum, and their sustenance depends on its continued influence, why should the members of that stratum sacrifice their own interests and position *except* as necessary to placate incipient insurgency? Values require a philosophical validation that goes beyond a brute contest of power, to be sure, but that validation only reinforces their hold. If egalitarianism, as construed by those alienated from or only loosely tied to the present social system, urges a redistribution of income for their benefit, why should the many more who support the system consent to a reinterpretation of the distributive value which penalizes them? Perhaps some social-welfare measures are warranted to make the system work better, to improve equality of opportunity (as Rainwater's Boston sample seems to say), but not to replace the value of distribution according to earned rewards.

Moreover, the professional politicians who cannot ignore the massed (largely urban-massed) demands of those who want to be cut into the system's goodies, also cannot ignore the demands of those who provide those goodies. As mediators of the balance of power in society, the politicians must be responsive to those on whose power they rely to keep the system functioning. Like most mediators, they are able to persuade the resisters that some concessions will redound to their benefit, will oil the system's squeaky wheels, and will make the whole function more smoothly. But given the disconnection between government spending and government income, and the enormous complex of legislation applying to a maze of social relationships, the professional politicians do not always mediate under conditions of partisan confrontation. The system operators make their own demands for the more effective functioning of the system, and the politicians—responsive to their needs, as indeed they must be—review those demands sympathetically, often affirmatively. But the result—not necessarily intended either by business and its allies, or by the politicians who respond to them—may be to preserve (roughly, not precisely) the existing distribution of rewards in society.

Power is thus used to support interests with which the good of the nation is identified, without any intention of hurting or depriving any other group. Business groups argue for a tax credit to spur investment, from which society as a whole will benefit (even though some will benefit more than others). Construction unions seek support for more building (from which some home and apartment dwellers will benefit but which will also shore up and even boost construction wages and construction costs). Local and state politicians defend local discretion in the use of federally shared revenues, and most of such revenues find their way into activities wanted by middle-class majorities. The tax "system" is compounded by a variety of taxes on income, consumption, and payrolls. The income tax has extensive "schedules" indicating what is to be considered as income, what deducted, and what given special treatment. Each of these items is negotiated, and each, generally, without respect to any total effect. But when the effect of all individual taxes is added together, the average toll is virtually the same over most of the income distribution— between 20 and 25 percent of income.[6] The principle of progressivity, on which redistributive (egalitarian) programs rely, gets lost in the complex bargaining. Resistance to more progressive tax rates may not even have to be mobilized, merely expected, so that the prospect of unfavorable reaction deters any increased levies on upper incomes. Joseph Pechman, a leading tax economist, has said: "Politicians find it useful to support progression in principle, but then turn to regressive sources when new revenue needs arise." [7] Payroll taxes, one of the most regressive forms, have risen steadily until they now produce 30 percent of federal revenue.

Influence on public policy is not the only means by which above-average income receivers can protect themselves from redistributive effects. Many—not all—occupy positions of private discretionary power which permit them to recover at least part of the amounts that inflation might have redistributed away. Business retains control over its prices, except for those limited periods when the government has desultorily played with price controls, so that higher costs can be recouped in higher prices. Labor unions negotiate not only wage increases but cost-of-living escalators to preserve the value of their gains. The unions' power to advance and protect the interests of their members is linked to business's power to raise its prices. In neither case can it be argued that such action is "inequitable." Who expects business to go on absorbing higher costs? Who would argue that workers should not benefit from greater productivity or remain silent and complacent if their real income falls? But in both cases the effect is to recover—"compensate for"—the higher costs of full employment and welfare.

Professional people set their own scale of remuneration, even with respect to services provided under social programs. (Medicaid and Medicare provide medical benefits to low-income groups, but in the process vastly expand the incomes of the medical profession.) As larger appropriations are needed to fund programs, inflationary pressures grow, and compensating actions are taken, by those powerful enough to preserve their "position."

The upward movement of incomes and prices proceeds unevenly, raggedly, spasmodically. The actions of federal and state legislatures, city councils, corporate price setters, collective negotiators, small shopkeepers and scattered professionals can scarcely be coordinated. In the jerky ascent, first one group and then another feels left behind, and uses whatever private discretion or political pressure it can muster to improve its position. In the process almost all groups, at one time or another, are bound to feel that their circumstances have deteriorated, or when their relative loss has been roughly compensated for to feel that its recaptured "equity" is nibbled away all too quickly. Everyone seems to lose periodically, no one seems to benefit permanently, but over time, a period of years, the relative position of most income groups is not sharply affected. The egalitarian pressure is not without effect. Everyone wins some claim to an income, and the concept of a social minimum income, below which no one should fall, makes headway. But this redistributive effect is itself eroded even if not erased by the reluctance—often the unwitting reluctance—of upper-income groups to transfer any substantial amount of real resources to those whose needs they detachedly recognize.

The resulting inflationary momentum is not the familiar wage-price spiral of economic theory. That spiral is, so to speak, all "within the family." This is a redistributive spiral, an egalitarian spiral, involving a dialectic between the establishment (corporations and their ancillaries, including the unions) and the disestablished or unassimilated.

Occasionally the conflict between the privileged and the excluded becomes direct, overt. In 1972, Local 46 of the Metallic Lathers Union, New York City, was ordered by a federal court to open its ranks by issuing 250 "work permits"—the term itself reveals a locus of power—annually for three years, half to whites, half to minorities. The union's unskilled jobs paid approximately $400 a week (in 1974), and the number of applicants was too large to be accommodated. Said one of the unlucky, the disestablished speaking to the established: "What are we supposed to do now, crawl back into the earth?" [8]

But the disjointed nature of the whole decision-making process, both public and private, generally allows for a more anonymous conflict—anger directed at symbols ("Wall Street") and abstractions ("business"). Indeed, some might not even recognize themselves among the protagonists, or at times might even conceive themselves to be on the opposing rather than defending side. Labor unions, for example, though bargaining opponents of managements and often vitriolic in their denunciations, are actually defending the same territory, even if not always in the same sector. If they have also served as champions for populist causes which would appear to undermine their positions of relative privilege (relative, that is, to those seeking greater equality), this is due in part to their ability to protect themselves from the effects of those causes. There is no more ardent champion of the most rigorous definition of full employment than organized labor, since the fuller employment is, the more advantageous, even if inflationary, are the conditions for bidding up the wages of its members. With somewhat less enthusiasm, union leaders also support social welfare programs, which will benefit some of their members and in any event may help to gratify protesting groups which otherwise might nibble away at job rights and privileges, or object to disproportionate union gains. (Labor unions and blacks have been in an ambiguous and ambivalent relationship, part hostile, part fraternal, for years.)

For a time it was hoped that economic growth would accommodate the new demands for "more," just as a half-century earlier economic growth had helped to meet the old demands for "more, more, more" (Samuel Gompers speaking on behalf of the labor movement). But the situations are basically dissimilar. The old dissidents were themselves contributing to the flow of goods of which they wanted a larger share. The new dissidents have been excluded from the production process and are sitting, for the most part, on the sidelines. They insist, nonetheless, on a larger share in the social wealth. In the older case, growth could finesse the issue of redistribution—everybody simply earned more. In the present situation, if growth is to contain protest, it must go hand in hand with redistribution. The issue cannot be finessed.

Even so, cannot the gains of economic growth be used to meet the demands of those who are left on the sidelines? If what is wanted is improvement in the lot of the disadvantaged, then, as Daniel Bell asks, "Why not . . . allow greater incentives for those who can expand the total social output and use this larger 'social pie' for the mutual (yet differential) advantage of all?" [9] The question is a fair one, but its answer is given in the resistance shown by those receiving greater incentives to a greater diversion of their income to the disadvantaged. Progressively higher marginal taxes somehow reduce to a common proportional average rate, and expenditures out of the revenues raised—even those which seem intended for the less fortunate—somehow wind up shared by those who are already fortunate. The social and political problems of effecting redistribution cannot be met by an arithmetic exercise.

Can public employment help to satisfy those whom the private sector cannot or will not assimilate? Insofar as the unassimilated are employable, of course it can, but it does little to counter inflationary pressures. Public production must not compete with private production, so it cannot contribute to the flow of goods and services which people are ready to pay for. Public services of a noncompetitive nature could long ago have been provided by expanding tax revenues, if taxpayers had wanted those services. The lament of the good-society idealist has been precisely that people prefer private consumption to public amenities. To sweep into public employment some who otherwise would have received unearned assistance—or no assistance—does nothing to increase the output of *wanted* goods, and—like assistance itself—increases the demand on those goods. Public employment may rescue the dignity of those whom it assimilates, but it does little or nothing to contain inflationary pressures. Indeed, public employment—the vastly expanded civil service in all government jurisdictions—is in process of becoming lumped, in the public view, with welfare, *both* regarded as a drain on the more productive private sector. To *reduce* the rolls of public employment, especially in the fiscally hard-pressed and minority-populated cities, has become the mark of civic and social responsibility to those who identify most closely with the prevailing economic system.

In sum, a new wave of egalitarian pressure has surfaced in the period since World War II, accentuated by its solidification in urban centers, where it is more visible, more vocal, and more politically potent. This pressure has elicited a response couched in the familiar terms of the American distributive value—achievement under conditions of equal opportunity—but equal opportunity has been redefined to require greater equality of actual circumstances. The professional politicians have had to mediate the terms of a new bargain between dissident minorities and a resistant majority. New concessions have been made with respect to employment and welfare, but the concessions have not been paid for with real money. In the system by which any actual income transfers are made, with a disconnection between government spending and income, it has been easy, and seemingly equitable, for many people to defend their own income positions while urging higher incomes for those with less. Any resulting gap between federal income and outgo has been met by the politically more expedient means of debt and inflation. "That was always our quandary," explains Donald M. Baker, one-time counsel to the Office of Economic Opportunity, "how could we alleviate poverty without hurting the people whose support we needed to alleviate poverty?" [10]

The pressures for redistribution and the defenses of existing distribution have both been partly accommodated by a variety of devices which disguise what is going on but contribute heavily to inflation. Some redistribution has occurred, but only by creating an environment of future uncertainties inimical to the functioning of the economic system. Almost a century and a half earlier Chevalier had foreseen a time when pressures for egalitarian concessions "would end by palsying the spirit of enterprise which has created the prosperity of the country." [11] Nor have the results been satisfying to those who feel rejected. "There is a real threat," warns Roger Wilkins of the *New York Times*'s editorial board, "that if America does not make real efforts to attend to some of her suffering people or to renew her ailing cities, a sad and irretrievable unraveling of her social fabric will occur." [12]

A ragged kind of polarization seems to be occurring that is destructive of social cohesion. On the one hand are those assimilated by the system, with varying degrees of attachment, who under the American constitutional and distributive values of competitive private achievement quite properly view society as a field of economic opportunity for their exploitation. On the other hand are those who have been excluded from or alienated by the system or are only marginally attached to it, and who see the society which has excluded them as fair game for their exploitation. (As the tenth century Syrian poet, al-Mutanabbi, wrote during the Age of Caliphs: "Unbroken drive/Even for welfare is only warfare.")

Arnold Cantor, an AFL-CIO researcher, has pinpointed the issue perceptively. "In discussing income distribution, few people question the need to alleviate the circumstance of the very poor. . . . To help those in the middle [Cantor's fellow unionists] and *at the same time* [my italics] bring more people into the 'middle' is a far more complicated task. The notion of fair shares then starts to dig deeply into all economic and social values, laws and institutions—the relationship between wages and profits, the role of collective bargaining, tax justice, public investment policies, resource allocation and government regulation.'' [13] It would be fair to add that many of Cantor's union members might feel unhappy at the prospect of a review of the role of collective bargaining and uneasy at the difficulty of helping themselves while helping those less fortunate, of having their own cake and letting others eat it too. But he is right about the complexity of the problem. Let us explore the complications further.

It would be patently erroneous to conclude that inflation occurs *only* because upper-income producers (workers, managers, financiers) seek to recapture income which would otherwise be redistributed away from them to nonproducers—the old and disabled, the unemployed, the welfare clients, or even to those in public employment. Such a conclusion would ignore the effects of the twentieth-century organizational revolution, which restructured the American economy in ways which permitted a different exercise of economic power. Before the Great Depression, power over economic decisions continued to accumulate in the hands of corporations. After the Great Depression the large corporations were joined by the large labor unions, the former both making concessions to and co-opting the latter. Those became the principal influences in a more organized and structured economic system.

In effect, competition in the twentieth century passed from an individualistic to an organized base. Organizations now competed for advantages. This was the outcome not of any sinister ambition or greed but of the very structure of values to which society subscribed. Vigorous individual competition meant losers as well as winners. The successful grew strong in their own success. The large corporation was the product of American push, given free play within the competitive system. One could enforce fair rules of the competitive game (regulatory legislation) but one could not put a limit on growth without jeopardizing the competitive game itself. Once this development had occurred, however, it was only a matter of time before the corollary became evident: organization was necessary to protect the individuals *within* the large corporations. Unions were recognized as the worker's alternative to serfdom (in the phrase of J. M. Clark), or as a countervailing power (as John Kenneth Galbraith put it). Corporate power was matched by labor power; competition continued on an organized as well as an individual basis. No less a partisan than John L. Lewis insisted only on the freedom of unions to compete in a private market system.

The mass unions of the post-World War II period can themselves be considered the product of egalitarian sentiment. The incomes of their members were regarded, in the reform spirit of the 1930s, as "too low," the result of the individual's weak competitive power relative to organized industry. Unionization was encouraged and protected to make competition—and incomes—more "equal." In an earlier day the corporation had been judicially granted the status of an individual, for most purposes. Now the same status was extended to labor unions. The belief in competitive individualism as the ethical basis for distributing the social product could thus be maintained, though the "individuals" might be General Motors and the Brotherhood of Teamsters.

The economic effects of organized competition could not be so easily accommodated. Since World War II strong unions have bargained and continue to bargain for substantial wage increases within a political and economic context that stresses full employment. Fiscal and monetary measures designed to curb the spread of unemployment whenever it manifests itself have the unintended effect of improving the unions' bargaining position relative to employers by sustaining the public's demand for the latter's output. Without unions, the upward pressures on wages would not be so organized or effective. Without a full employment policy, rising prices would curb demand, employment, and union wage pressures. With both unions and full employment measures, increases in production costs can be passed along in the form of higher prices.

119

Thus there are two interacting distributive influences, separate but related, propelling inflation in American society—an egalitarian movement which is both accommodated and resisted, and organized competition operating with the same freedom as individual competition in an earlier day.

The effect of the latter, like the effect of the former, is to modify the pattern of income distribution without radically transforming it. Despite the greater power of some unions over others, the network of competitive price relations among industries and firms is sufficiently stable and strong to prevent the wage relations, which they subsume, from creating their own independent patterns. Within uncertain limits, the system of prices constrains the system of wages. The superior competitive position (bargaining power) of a union or company may register once and then sustain its advantage, without providing repeated additional advantage. The respects in which all industries and major corporations are similarly affected by wage patterns, and demand levels, and ongoing technological change help to give persisting structure to wage and income relationships, even in the face of inflation, and even though dissimilarities in these conditions do subject that structure to stress and change. Some few categories of workers do benefit disproportionately from their collective power, but on the whole organizational competition provides an inflationary impetus without seriously disordering the income distribution.

We can, then, repeat our earlier observation. Wages, incomes, and prices move jerkily, unevenly, like the mechanical racehorses in a carnival sideshow. Now one is ahead, then another catches up. The bargains and price actions cannot be easily coordinated. The inflationary climate affects them all, accommodating monetary increases and at the same time draining away their value. No one is happy, even those who improve their position. Satisfaction with an above-average increase is offset by the months of unhappiness preceding it, when prices were rising while one's own income remained static.

As the price level moves up in this fashion, allocations for welfare recipients must of course be increased, and the number of those requiring assistance expands. The mechanics of the process which we previously examined resume their awkward operation. The larger allocations for the marginal populations are not financed by higher tax levies on those who are better off. Those people—themselves hit by inflation—are doing their best to maintain their economic position. They sigh for those who are in distress, believe that "government" should do more for those who deserve it, believe too that there are many spongers who do not merit aid, and resist any increase in taxes. The rising welfare allocations are financed by government debt, increasing the total of demands on the available supply of goods, and increasing prices. The cost-of-living clauses in collective agreements are triggered off, and wages in the organized sector heave a little, giving another little push to inflation. The two distributive influences—redistributive egalitarianism and organizational competition—continue to interact.

The upward movement, however, does not necessarily accumulate momentum, as economists once thought. Various resistances—of the domestic market, of international trade, of legislative action, of administrative monetary and fiscal policies—intervene to brake a climb which threatens to become precipitous. Nevertheless, the inflationary pressures are built into the system and its values to a degree which justifies an expectation of a continuing inflationary tendency. Moreover, temporary abatement of inflationary pressure is as likely as not to signal a worsening of the economic position of those most marginal to the system, with a consequent building up of frustration, despair, and anger, to erupt at some later date.

The complexity of the distributive value-problem is immensely compounded if we extend our vision from the domestic scene to the world stage. From that viewpoint, the United States as a nation—its disadvantaged and all—becomes to the developing nations the exploiter that has created an international order for its own benefit while reducing all other continents except Europe (Japan now an honorary "member") to the status of suppliers of resources and cheap labor, sometimes through imperialistic ventures, sometimes through the agency of multinational corporations. Egalitarian demands for redistributive "justice" are directed at the United States couched in terms of its own values. Writes Michael Manley, Prime Minister of Jamaica: "Ideals based on the belief in the equality of man ring as true in the ears of Jamaica's poor as they did to the framers of the American Declaration of Independence in 1776. Sooner or later these ideals are translated into more precise and demanding categories of economic expectation: jobs, food, housing." And, he adds, now speaking for the world's "permanent losers," if America lacks the will to respond, "there are nearly two billion poor people who will demand to know why not and who will be rapidly succeeded by three billion offspring who may just cease to ask questions at all." [14]

The insistence on a redistribution of world income has in recent years become more vocal and visible, just as in the case of similar domestic demands. The United Nations has provided a platform on which the hardships of poverty-stricken peoples can be paraded, lamented, and made the basis for rejecting the present international order. The more affluent nations have been made to feel guilty for their affluence. To placate countries which see themselves on the fringes of a world economic system run primarily for the benefit of others, the more affluent countries have extended aid in a variety of forms—grants, military assistance, credit at favorable rates. International agencies, largely financed by the wealthy nations, have likewise provided help. Credit has been forthcoming from the private multinational corporations. The total of all such transfers to the low-income countries has not been large, in comparison with world income, but it is concentrated on those goods moving in international channels. In addition, developing countries with control over the supply of certain resources, notably the oil-producing countries, have used that control to appropriate larger shares of world income, justifying their actions on egalitarian grounds.

This redistributive egalitarianism on the world scene has been coupled in the industrialized countries with the same phenomena that we have observed in the United States—organizational competition in a full-employment context, not always in the same form but with the same effect. Inflation afflicts all those countries from which the developing economies must import much of their minimal needs. The inflationary impact has been exacerbated by the reluctance of consumers in the wealthier countries, notably the United States, to forego consumption of world-traded goods even at high prices. The demands of the affluent increase the price to the poor. Thus the amount of additional real income flowing to the developing nations from those which dominate the international economy has been diluted; their circumstances (even for the fortunate few in command of strategic resources) have been improved less than expected, and disillusionment leads to shriller demands for equity. The international scene duplicates and extends the inflationary pressures on the domestic front.

Redistributive demands are not restricted to money. They extend to removal of those personal privileges and discretionary rights which have sanctioned discriminatory treatment in the past. Confining our attention to the domestic scene, we need only remind ourselves of some of the most recent attempts to redefine distributive justice. Public schools should be racially integrated, even if this requires transporting children to schools in a neighborhood other than their own. Admission to college should be open to all high school graduates, since reliance on grades may reflect prejudicial preparatory experience. Housing should be available to the poor in all areas, not simply the slums, even if this requires public subsidization of low-income housing located in middle-income neighborhoods or the invalidation of zoning laws which prescribe more acreage per home than low-income families can afford. Jobs should be awarded to individuals on the basis of the minimum qualifications needed to perform them rather than on the basis of some standard not demonstrably related to the job, such as a diploma or a degree. Employers should hire and unions should admit to membership minority peoples in roughly the same proportion they bear to the total population. Corporations should be obliged to conform to minority hiring quotas in all grades of employment.

This drive for equality—whether of opportunity or condition—obviously calls for active governmental intervention in private institutions. Government agents must monitor private behavior, challenge it if considered discriminatory on its face, file suits in federal courts, and threaten loss of government contracts—in short, employ coercive force to elicit private actions which would not otherwise be forthcoming. The challenge is not only to the prevailing distributive value but to the constitutional value as well.

Harvey Brooks, who sees redistribution as a vast exercise in "social engineering," requiring "new kinds of 'hard' technology," reduces the matter to a simple formula. "The citizens of a single nation are equal before the law, and this creates the major pressure for economic equality as well." [15] But this simplistic statement unlocks a major philosophical dilemma. Democratic egalitarianism has been defended on the premise that it provides equal freedom, equal opportunity, for the individual—one man, one vote, without respect to property qualifications, educational attainment, or even literacy. But if this political equality is then *used* to achieve economic equality, it does so only through coercion. Political equality is revealed as democratic only in the numbers it favors, not in the principle it invokes. The tyranny of the majority differs from the tyranny of a minority only in an arithmetic sense, not in any categorical way. This squares with Tocqueville's perception that democracy reduces to equality and that people will surrender freedom rather than equality. Authoritarianism in the pursuit of equality thus wins the name of democracy. "People's democracies" in Russia, China, and elsewhere can use that term in this (but to us peculiar) sense.

If this is so, it is true with respect to the redistribution of income no less than to the redistribution of privilege. In Bertrand de Jouvenel's words, "The more one considers the matter, the clearer it becomes that redistribution is in effect far less a redistribution of free income from the richer to the poorer, as we imagined, than a redistribution of power from the individual to the State." [16]

We have already asked the question: If demands for redistribution lead to partial concession but also firm resistance, with resulting inflation, which is the cause—the challenge or the response?

Challenges to the Distributive Value

To this we can now add a second question: If demands for redistribution of income or of privilege are thwarted and those thwarted then invoke coercive authority on their behalf, who is to blame for the coercion—those who challenge, or those who resist? And if the possibility of a more authoritarian government (threatening the prevailing constitutional value based on autonomy, freedom of contract, and rights of property) emerges from the egalitarian thrust, would it be surprising if those whose distributive interests are endangered should scuttle their own constitutional value and use their power to install a government more responsive to them, rather than subject themselves to coercion on behalf of others?

IV

IN THE FACE OF
CHALLENGE

11

Social Values Declining

THE UNITY of a society ultimately depends on its sense of community. A commonalty of feelings holds people together. Numerous unwritten laws of conduct, patterns of culture, codes of behavior, and expectancies of appropriate relationships are learned in childhood and during maturation. These collectively constitute a kind of rough consensus as to the obligations which every member owes to every other member in a variety of commonly encountered circumstances. The obligations need not be identical for all, but they must be reciprocal, so that the significant *relationships* are provided for. Above all they must be generally accepted.

This network of contingent social obligations—activated as circumstances dictate—ultimately derives from the social values. The understanding of what one may "properly" say about others, or to others, of appropriate behavior when one encounters others (friends or strangers) on the street, in public rooms, or in one's own home, derives from our learned views of how far the autonomy and equality of the individual extends and what kinds of behavior toward others the society constrains. We also learn under what circumstances youth defers to age (in some instances) and age to youth (in others), men to women and women to men, citizens to public authorities and public authorities to citizens, and so on in a variety of roles and relationships. Thus, aside from defining the more fundamental relations among people—their legal rights and privileges, their freedoms and immunities, the underlying purposes which infuse the whole body of law—social values also define the proprieties of a people. These behavioral obligations, like the social values, change with changes in objective conditions.

The cities have always experienced most urgently the need for constraining personal autonomy by a sense of social obligation. The more that people crowd together, the more inescapable become new constraints on individual conduct. Since changes in customary patterns of conduct are often difficult to effect without some codification, laws regulating personal behavior increase. Cities pass rules providing for compulsory forms of sanitation in private homes and public institutions, for zoning restrictions, and for limitations on the use of automobiles. There are also regulations concerning smoking in public, on the number of people permitted in enclosed spaces, housing codes, and use of the streets and of the parks. The catalogue could be extended indefinitely. Population density limits personal freedoms.

More than density is involved. The large central cities of the United States ceased their growth some years ago, but the populations residing within them (even the poverty groups) have more goods with which to occupy the same amount of space. The number of television sets and transistor radios escalates, and noise levels must be controlled. The automobile culture proliferates, with attendant controls on driver licensing, behavior in traffic, parking, insurance, and car inspection. Medical facilities expand, and the greater clientele requires a more regulated—bureaucratic—service. Entertainment—private and public—becomes a growth industry, its varieties and styles affecting whole neighborhoods, again raising a need for regulation.

The public controls over private behavior, due to both density and affluence, are so necessary that despite initial differences over their specific content they quickly come to be accepted. Consensus follows common need. At least that has tended to be the pattern until recent years.

The post-World War II concentrations of blacks in the cities, and their growing sense of cohesive power in the face of continuing discrimination, has altered what was a general concurrence on social obligations. Disbelief in social values had led to disrespect for social obligations. Confronted with the evident denial of equal opportunities, dissident factions of the black community, particularly among the young, have responded by making their own opportunities out of a disregard for the generally accepted contingent social obligations. The network of interdependencies created by density and affluence provides countless ways in which those who are alienated by the society can get back at that society, by flouting its conventions and laws and by disrupting social order. That many blacks are themselves the victims of such behavior is simply a by-product of the underlying alienation from white-controlled society. The major cities, most dependent on consensus for their very continuity as centers of a culture, become the most vulnerable targets when obligations to maintain order are rejected.

This racial division is, of course, not the only source of urban difficulties. In previous chapters we have observed other challenges to present social values, from which any sense of social obligations must derive. Nevertheless, the racial cleavage—the "two societies" of the National [Kerner] Commission on Civil Disorders and the "deepening division" of the National Commission on the Causes and Prevention of Crime—is clearly at the heart of the matter. The disaffections of the affluent or idealistic young, and of white workers pressed by inflation and taxes, are at best contributing causes.

The problem of America's cities highlights the present state of America's social values. The decline of the latter is most evident in the decline of the former. And yet, to this proposition a demurrer may be entered by pointing to similar problems being encountered by other societies around the world. If not racial conflict, then comparable confrontation based on ethnic, religious, or language differences are to be discerned in countries as dissimilar as Canada and Uganda, Malaysia and Rhodesia, Belgium and Yugoslavia, Ireland and Lebanon, Trinidad and Spain, Cyprus and the Philippines—but why extend the list further? Each day's news brings fresh or recurring instances. The generality of these subgroup confrontations suggests either that social values are breaking down all over, or that something other than the breakdown of societal values is at work in the world at large. In either case, it would appear that the problems America faces, most sharply delineated in its cities, are not peculiar to it.

There is considerable validity to this view. Our preoccupation with social values in America has restrained us from considering social values in other countries. While each society's values are unique in their entirety—an identity different from all other social identities—there are nevertheless similarities in some of the component parts. In particular, most countries in the world today are being challenged on their distributive value. On this score America is not unique, but for significant reasons America is being challenged on that value to a degree which is unique.

It does appear that something approximating Tocqueville's continuing, relentless surge toward equality, so long confined to the West, has now spread to the rest of the world. Societies which for centuries have accepted inequality as part of their system of social values—notably, but not only, in Asia—are now infected with the egalitarian virus. Among the reasons for this phenomenon are increased exposure to the West as a result of World War II; expanded communications; increased tourism; the influence of international governments and agencies; the anti–colonialist movement; the cold war; improvements in education and living standards which spawned new leaderships; and the stimulus of example. For these and other reasons those groups that have been denied equality have sought to achieve it. And those possessing special advantages—such groups exist in every society—have attempted to retain them, or as much of them as possible, by the only means possible: concession, co-optation, and repression. Where divisions deepen and animosities harden, the first two devices lose their effectiveness. If relied on to soothe dissatisfactions which can only be satisfied by equality, they require the advantaged groups to surrender too much. The only fall-back is repression, inviting retaliation, thus bringing about escalation on both sides.

This is the world-wide phenomenon, whether the challenge is raised in societies already professing egalitarianism, such as the United States, or in societies which have valued the greater stability provided by distributive arrangements grounded in a status system into which one is born. This is the world-wide phenomenon of which America partakes.

But the situation in the United States is exacerbated by its own special circumstances. Foremost is its deep-seated emotional belief in equality of opportunity, and the consequent sense of guilt by those who deny it in practice—by whatever sophistries the practices are justified, by whatever psychological devices the sense of guilt is smothered. America has been regarded as an upstart by countries with far longer histories, but in its devotion to the egalitarian faith it is a patriarch among nations. Other countries, even socialist socie-ties, are still struggling to endow their egalitarian creeds with a devo-tional belief that comes easily to most Americans. But it is the very strength of this conviction that makes equally ingrained prejudices and pretensions so much more difficult to admit, and hence to re-move. The internal conflict can as readily be handled by a vigorous and self-reassuring assertion of the rightness of one's prejudices as by a recognition that such prejudices are incompatible with a social value too deeply held to be abandoned. The consequence is a white society which moves spasmodically towards revising its institutions to reflect its egalitarian beliefs, but whose will to persist fails with a recurring realization of the advantages it would have to abandon if all discriminatory lines were eradicated—above all the sense of identity (and in this case superiority) which is partly secured through an exclusivist restriction on eligibility for membership in a kinship group. If ecumenicism has proved an elusive goal, universal consanguinity is an even more difficult achievement.

Compounding the American problem is that post-World War II phenomenon we noted earlier. Like mammoth organisms the cities have inhaled blacks and exhaled whites. Mobilization in such compact masses provides political bargaining power which cannot be ignored. As blacks move into control of the public school systems, black youngsters will most certainly not be indoctrinated with the social values of the white society which has demeaned them. It is not easy to imagine black teachers infusing into black children that belief in the existence of equal opportunity which became religion to youngsters in Marquand's version of Clyde, Mass. The divide seems almost sure to deepen.

The resulting impasse may be a protracted one, its resolution delayed for a long and indefinite time. But delayed resolution only sets the stage for continuing decline in the hold which present social values have on American society, and in their effectiveness in holding that society together.

Of course social values need not deteriorate uniformly. All challenges to them are not equally pressing. It is on the distributive value that American society is clearly being pressed most urgently. Nevertheless, the values are interrelated, and one cannot be challenged without involving the others. We have already seen how distributional questions inescapably involve constitutional issues. Not very far down the road it seems equally evident that the problems of resource supply and growth effects, both domestic and international, will likewise be drawn into the picture, threatening our present focal value.

The weakening of the value structure necessarily involves an erosion of business influence, which has been the root of America's social values. The branches cannot be cleaved without affecting the root itself. The use by business leadership of further concessions and co-optation as instruments for preserving its primum position would be subjected to a dual handicap. Not only would it have made so many concessions that it would be reluctant to dilute its position further; it would also have made so many concessions that to make more would lose it the respect and confidence of its own bureaucracy, perhaps even betray its *self*-confidence. The ebullience, vigor, and brashness which have characterized its chief protagonists in the past would evaporate into mists of uncertainty and confusion.

If this state of affairs continued, business would in time become simply one among a number of contending interests, which professional politicians would attempt to hold together by mediation. Government would become a Mother Hubbard, concerned only with keeping unruly offspring in some semblance of order.

Since the weakening of *social* values has the inevitable effect of driving people back into their *group* identities—ethnic, racial, vocational and functional, to a lesser extent religious and geographic —the necessary consequence is value diffuseness. Divergences between group interests are exaggerated, commonalty dissolves into particularity. The withdrawal of people from the disorder of general society into more cohesive and insular units functions as a form of security. The stress on group uniqueness heightens the sense of belonging, identity, exclusiveness. It also increases the potential for intergroup conflict at sensitive points of contact.

If these retreats into group identity are already evident, they would intensify in a state of continuing drift. The position of mediating politicians would be rendered more and more difficult in the absence of an underlying commonalty of values, held in place by a dominant institution asserting its leadership with confidence and accepted— however subject to criticism—as broadly representative of social purpose. The politicians would confront a scene of contentious interests, each demanding a larger share of the social product and reinforcing its demand by whatever powers it could muster, regardless of the impact on the social structure. Demands for "representation" in all sorts of decision-making bodies, from corporate boards to prison boards, would be forthcoming from all the major groups, on the ground that no one else could properly bespeak their interests.

Faced with such diverse pressures, confronted by a succession of crisis situations requiring opportunistic resolution, the credibility of professional politicians would be subject to erosion. The neutrality of the political power brokers would be questioned, and favoritism and bias charged when one interest group or another failed to achieve some strategic demand. The task of holding together such a patchwork of conflicting pressure groups would undermine the political process itself.

Such a makeshift state of pluralist-particularist interests, relating to each other by tenuous links which now might be snapped and now repaired with difficulty, could continue for an indefinite time. Protracted periods of disorder have been known before. The chaotic conditions could also create an opportunity which some more spirited politician might exploit to his own advantage, eschewing a mediatorial role and setting up himself or a party as the force for order, a political anchor in time of national drift, a monolith of strength in contrast to the institutional shards on the social landscape. Partly imposed on and partly accepted by a disillusioned and exhausted public, even an authoritarian government might seem preferable to continuing disorder and danger.

Until or unless such a demagogic force—or a thruster group—emerged, internal or external, threads of the former common values and the shadow of the Hobbesian fear of a war of each against all would prevent a completer disintegration of society. The sense of community within the larger whole would be lost, its function weakly served by a common sense of the greater danger of total disunity. But past some point of decline, a restoration of social values could not be expected. Changes in objective conditions would prevent their being put back in place, and their erosion would make them less acceptable. However fragile a basis for social cohesion, they would have to serve in their fractured state until replaced.

This chilling prospect, or some similar version, is by no means just a fantasy of despairing intellectuals who have lost faith in America. It constitutes a grim possibility which may conceivably unfold from the changing objective conditions around us. Nevertheless, the process and its end result are by no means fatalistically determined. Changing conditions can be met and acted upon to produce different results. It is as though American society were in the position of Dickens's Scrooge confronting the Ghost of Christmas Yet to Come and asking if these things must be, and hearing the Spirit reply, "Unless . . ."

12

Can Social Values
Be Preserved?

THE STRATEGY for coping with social and economic challenges which is most congenial to the American system is incrementalism. Incrementalism can be defined as piecemeal modification of institutions and practices in response to the felt necessities of the times, a kind of economic counterpart of the political common-law process. Its intent is to combine continuity with improvement, conservatism with reform, gradualism with evolutionary development. It aims at more of the same, but better—as, for example more production will give us the means of solving poverty and pollution.

Karl Popper has elaborated, in *The Open Society and Its Enemies,* the philosophical basis for preferring this responsive, patchwork social renovation to a more sweeping systems approach. Wrenched out of its extended analysis of the uncertainty of knowledge as the basis for action and the unknowability of future reality, Popper's argument reduces to the preferability of small moves rather than major programs. Particular policies can be instituted with less social upheaval than radical reform requires, and can be more easily modified if they go astray. Any adverse unintended consequences of purposive action—to use Robert Merton's phrase—can be minimized.

Reform may proceed at pedestrian pace, but there is less likelihood of stumbling. Modification in bits and pieces—marginal adjustment—permits an easier if more ragged accommodation of divergent interests. Consensus is preserved through continuous implicit (sometimes explicit) bargaining in both the private and public spheres.

It is readily understandable why business leaders would prefer this incremental approach to social problems. Since they and their predecessors have been the dominant influence in designing the present system, they are uninterested in any major transformation. The complaints—the challenges—are heard, both by them and by the professional politicians who must mediate between the challengers and those challenged. But the system modifications which are made as concessions are limited to modest, remedial, step-by-step measures which preserve the system and the social values which help to keep it in place.

Challenges often originate as vocal but inarticulate protests from a group or class of people who are aggrieved by what the "system" does to them or fails to do for them. However, their voice is heard and an argument on their behalf shaped and sharpened by intellectuals—idealists and reformers—who contrive solutions and demand reforms. The proposed solutions and reforms are often more sweeping than the problem requires, since the intellectual predisposition is to push ideas to a theoretical conclusion. Unless such demands are resisted—the incrementalist argument goes—society is disrupted by ill-conceived social experimentation. The preferable course is to preserve social unity by meeting protest with moderate, limited concession. Any change is socially disturbing, and major change only creates new challenges.

This justification for incrementalism was expounded almost a century ago by Andrew Carnegie, with reference to the labor disturbances of 1886. "Our professors and political economists and the whole school of pessimists who tremble for the safety of human society in general, and of the Republic in particular, and the ministers that have boldly essayed to revolutionize existing conditions," he wrote, had found their "excitable natures" unnecessarily exercised.

Can Social Values Be Preserved?

Labor peace had already returned, so the reformers could look for another subject for "their anxious fears and forebodings." "Present conditions," said Carnegie, "have grown up slowly, and can be changed for the better only slowly and by small, successive steps." [1]

Carnegie's realist-optimist philosophy supports a political strategy of "muddling through." There have been hard times in the past—but here we still are. If one is inclined to hand wringing, there are always those to keen him on—Carnegie's professors, ministers, and intellectuals. "This moment is so on the brink of things. Overpopulation combined with a breakdown of food has wrecked the checks and balances of the industrialized world. In ten years we may be cavemen snatching the last bit of food from each other's mouths amid the stinking ruins of our cities, or we may be slaving—antlike—in some utterly systematized world where the individual will be utterly crushed that the mob (or the princes) may live. Every written word should be thought of as possibly the last that humanity will ever write . . ." [2] The anguished words sound as though written yesterday, but in fact they were penned by John Dos Passos more than fifty years ago. And here we still are, still surviving, still muddling through—and still hearing the same prophecies of doom from contemporary Jeremiahs. Such reminders tend to scuttle the bleak warning of impending disaster heard from would-be reformers, tend to undermine the challenges raised to a system which—whatever its defects (which can be remedied)—works better than any other of which there is *experience*. Incrementalism is simple American pragmatism, rooted in the American tradition. So goes the argument.

Since Carnegie's day, this process of slow, cautious, and modest reform has been reenforced by the increasing sophistication of corporate leaders. They are more inclined to give a little than resist a lot, easing tensions. In the face of criticism from vocal minorities that they have ignored the impact of their manufacturing operations on the environment, some companies have established board committees and staff vice presidents charged with evaluating and improving corporate policies in this respect. Challenged with discrimination against blacks and other minorities and against women,

139

corporations, especially in the major cities, have eased more women and blacks upward in the organizational hierarchy and have substantially increased their numbers—and visibility—at the lower job levels. Some companies have experimented with a "social audit" to accompany the financial statements. All have shown a greater sensitivity to public relations. With becoming candor they acknowledge that, in advancing society's welfare, *we* have all done less well than we can and *we* can do better if *we* pull together.

Government actions, if sometimes more dramatic, have been of the same order, seeking to placate the discontented without endangering the system itself—preservation through accommodation. Regulatory agencies have multiplied, and with them corresponding corporate bureaucracies—institutional modification. The result has been to complicate the conduct of business—more so for the smaller firms than for the large corporations which have assimilated the new requirements into their compartmentalized organization structure. But annoying though the regulations resulting from the increasing complexity of society may be, business itself is not without power to shape their form and implementation. The regulations—piecemeal and confined within the existing institutional context—preserve and refine the basic values (materialism, autonomy, competitive achievement) rather than attack them.

This incrementalist policy is by no means offensive to the public at large. Given the fact that so many people have their identities defined by the corporate system and subscribe to its values, it is safe to conclude that they prefer to avoid major institutional change, involving vast unknowns, if there is any prospect that minor progam changes will make the present system work a little better. If the challenges to our prevailing values can be successfully met by adaptation rather than by redesign, so much the better.

But *there* lies the real issue. *Can* marginal adjustments meet the challenges of the times? How long can a society continue to muddle through? Perhaps Dos Passos's despair was unwarranted in 1920, but maybe only the timing was off. After all, at the time he wrote, one World War had just been concluded, an even more savage one lay ahead (after an intervening world-wide depression greater than any previously known), to be followed by war in Korea, war in Vietnam, war in the Middle East, famine still stalking, American cities in shambles. Was Dos Passos so wrong? The thought strikes and then remains to haunt: Does incrementalism simply save, by tempering, a system which cannot help but create the unwanted effects?

R. H. Tawney believed that to be the case. Writing in the same year that Dos Passos had expressed his forebodings, Tawney spoke witheringly of those who believe that the existing social system (in England as in the United States) could be improved by pursuing the old channels more vigorously. Looking for a firmer economic foundation for social welfare, such meliorists "repeat, like parrots, the word productivity, because that is the word that rises first in their minds," regardless of the fact that productivity has already been accelerating as fast as economic discontent. Touched by compassion for the poor, whose misery they would alleviate, they fail to see that poverty is a product—fundamental and incorrigible—of the social order to which they cling.[3]

If incrementalism simply involves modest concessions to preserve the thrust of a flawed system, how can it be said to meet challenges to the system itself? The chief supporters of the American system, our corporate executives, are trained to turn away wrath. As Melville Dalton, a student of the managerial process, has elaborated, major executives are great compromisers. Estopped from one line of development, they pursue another. Opposed, they plan strategy which often involves seeking cooperation from others, which is gained through concessions. The same can be said of the professional politicians, whose function is to keep the system working. But the purpose of such expert broken-field running is still to win the same game—it involves no change of direction, no new goal. Challengers wanting to play a different game are unlikely to be impressed.

The French sociologist Michel Crozier, observing the contemporary scene, has expressed his disillusionment with the incrementalist policy. Like Popper, he rejects global, utopian reform, which embodies an arrogance of superficial knowledge. But he rejects, too, incrementalism, as ending up in blind escalation. He argues the need for changing not policies, not system, but direction. Avoid the hubris of fashioning a new social blueprint, eschew the complacency of doing more of the same but a little better, attempt instead to reorient existing institutions to achieve new objectives. Make love, not war, said youthful opponents of Vietnam. Change directions, not the system, says Crozier.

If some are gloomy about the prospects of incrementalism, Robert Nisbet is not one to comfort them. To him, incrementalism is all that can be expected from *any* social system. A system does not incorporate mechanisms for replacing itself. A little tinkering is *all* that can be expected. If that is not good enough, then change will have to come from outside the system. "Significant change is overwhelmingly the result of non-developmental [non-evolutionary, non-incremental] factors; that is to say, factors inseparable from external events and intrusions." [4]

The basic question then repeats itself: Can incrementalism *meet* challenges to present social values, when those include challenges to the very principles on which our basic institutions are premised? Will our corporate system (which includes most of us)—*can* our corporate system—change directions to pursue other values than materialism, private autonomy, and competitive achievement? If not, then incrementalism may not be an answer.

Another strategy for coping with challenges to the system and for preserving social values which support it is decentralization. The excesses of large-scale institutionalized behavior—impersonal, hierarchic, efficient by standards imposed by authority external to a locality, transcending interests closest to home—such excesses can be curbed by reasserting home rule. If power is exercised by people who are subject to it, if there is a more active participation in decision making by those who must live by those decisions, then there are likely to be fewer adverse consequences, and any unintended effects can be more readily removed.

The philosophy behind decentralization is historically rooted in the American constitutional system, with its reliance on sovereignty of the people: power devolves to the people in the smallest political units capable of dealing with any given problem. There is a transfer of authority upward only to the extent that a smaller unit (or a majority of such smaller units) concedes this to be necessary. The system is one of reserved powers. Thus Tocqueville notes: "In America the people form a master who must be obeyed *to the utmost limits of possibility.*" [5]

But if political decentralization was the rule at the time of Tocqueville's first visit in 1832, it was a badly battered rule when an acute English observer, James Bryce, surveyed the scene fifty years later. "The special advantages of local government have to a large extent vanished from the American States of today," he wrote.[6] Moreover, the centralization which Bryce observed as occurring in public life was taking place in the private governments of corporations as well. National businesses were absorbing local family firms, company policy was being formulated in New York or Chicago or some other metropolitan center and applied to local plants as to satrapies. Company decisions which affected the welfare of communities were being made without the latter having anything to say about them.

Nevertheless, the idea of popular sovereignty through decentralization was too deeply implanted to die out. It became a principle to be invoked at times on behalf of reform, as when "states' rights" were relied on to permit experimentation with social legislation, and at times on behalf of inaction, for example, to strike down federal innovations in social legislation. In the face of contemporary challenges to social values, it is not surprising that the principle of popular sovereignty through decentralization of power should be resuscitated as a strategy for dealing with those challenges. Nor is it surprising that the principle has been affirmed at times as a means of conserving and strengthening the traditional values and at times as an instrument for changing them. Those in the former category see the reinvigoration of home rule as a way of turning back to Tocqueville's America, reversing the bureaucratizing trend of the intervening years. There is an unspoken nostalgia for a simpler society, a yearning to recapture Percival Goodman's sense of "natural community," an integral *whole* society where people in face-to-face proximity act together "to protect and enhance the commonly held values," through slow, organic growth rather than through rationalized, systematized planning.[7] Neighborhood and community corporations have been proposed to oversee self-development programs.[8] Political scientist Norton Long urges that cities reestablish themselves as cooperative devices for their inhabitants "to pool their resources and meet their needs."[9]

Decentralization as a conserving strategy has not been confined to academic discussion. It has been politically employed in ways explicitly designed to meet some of the challenges generated by the system's performance. President Johnson's "war on poverty" had as one of its most controversial features provision for the "maximum feasible participation" of the poverty groups to be benefited. "Community Action Programs" sprouted all over the country as a result. The federal revenue-sharing policy inaugurated by President Nixon under his "New Federalism" raises and returns sizeable sums to state and local governments for their largely unrestricted use. Cities have decentralized their public school system to local community boards.

Decentralization of authority as a means of facilitating more active involvement in decision-making has also been advocated for the private government of the corporation. Abram Chayes, professor of law at Harvard University, has argued the desirability of viewing the corporation as an economic community in whose governance all its constituent groups have a voice. His then colleague, Kingman Brewster, likewise rejected centralism as a solution to present social problems and asserted the principle that "socially constructive energies will be released in the long run if problems can be attacked by and left to the final decision of those living closest to them." While reaffirming a belief in the desirability of dispersing power by leaving economic initiative in private (corporate) hands, Brewster suggested that to insure continued public acceptance of such private exercise of power, corporate behavior be subjected to political tests of a constitutional nature, not simply the economic test of the market. "In order to preserve the noneconomic values of pluralism as a social and political species of organization it is necessary to assure the political as well as the economic acceptability of corporate 'sovereignty.' '' [10] Corporate federalism takes a dignified place alongside traditional state federalism as an instrument of decentralized decision-making, providing it is made more responsible.

Corporate decentralization has not been only a verbal exercise. There has been a widespread voluntary devolution of authority to local managers in the expectation that they can be more responsive to local conditions. More notably, legislation has provided for collective bargaining by workers (industrial democracy), with a consequent network of collective agreements which have the effect of reinforcing the corporate system by making it more acceptable. Concessions to labor unions have won a sturdier support for prevailing social values than did the repressive campaigns waged by managements in the years prior to World War II. More recently there has been legislative and administrative provision for freer access by stockholders to corporate proxy machinery (shareholder democracy), which—even with almost certain defeat for protesting shareholders—has created an effective means for airing their protests at a public hearing, sometimes with the result of modifying corporate behavior. A new sense of responsibility by institutional investors for the actions of the corporations in which they invest has bolstered this resort to proxy voting. Again, modest corporate concessions in response to such internal pressures have strengthened rather than weakened the hold of prevailing values in American society.

As mentioned previously, some enthusiasts of decentralization see in such a strategy a means not of preserving existing values but of changing them. In this more apocalyptic version of decentralization, "communities" emerge not as the instruments for restoring the purity of traditional American values but as a thruster group bent on radical reform, in particular espousing a greater concern for nonmaterial interests. Focal and constitutional values thus come under the most direct attack, but the distributive value is also involved, since the present emphasis on competitive achievement would threaten the sense of community, and gross differences in economic circumstances would undermine social cohesion.

One of the most eloquent spokesmen on behalf of this strategy is Theodore Roszak, who advocates "deurbanization"—"cities should be thinned down and scaled out." Optimistically he believes that pressures are pushing in this direction: "How can one doubt that the communities will continue to push their way up like wildflowers through every crack in the suffocating pavements?" [11] E. F. Schumacher chides our "idolatry of giantism" and invokes the concept of optimum size ("for every activity there is a certain appropriate scale") to justify his belief that the upper limit on the size of a city should be 500,000 inhabitants. Scaling down the political unit provides more "intimate contact with actual people," a greater opportunity for self-realization and fulfillment. [12] Vine Deloria, Jr., advocate of a new tribalism for American Indians, seeks more generally to revive "the warm communal and familial bonds of traditional societies." [13] Robert Heilbroner foresees the possibility "that a post-industrial society would also turn in the direction of many pre-industrial societies—toward the exploration of inner states of experience rather than the outer world of fact and material accomplishment. . . . The struggle for individual achievement, especially for material ends, is likely to give way to the acceptance of communally organized and ordained roles." [14]

Despite the ardor of its advocates, there are good grounds for skepticism concerning the effectiveness of decentralization. Decentralization can work only within a society where there already exists widespread agreement on the basic values. While it is a strategy designed to permit innovation and variety, it is innovation and variety within an accepted framework. When the unifying social values themselves are being challenged, decentralization becomes a formula for *disintegrating* society.

This result may be intended, as a prelude to some projected reconstruction. But decentralized, autonomous units—while potentially disruptive of a larger society—are not a viable means for creating any society larger than their own, *if* they are to remain autonomous.

Here enters the fundamental weakness of decentralization as a strategy either of preserving existing values under challenge or inculcating new ones.

However much autonomy is returned to local and functional groups, there remain problems which can only be handled in a larger universe. These are often the most urgent problems, sometimes involving survival itself. If one community, in its local discretion, opted for nuclear power without adequate safety provisions, it would endanger more than itself. *Common* control within a wider geographical area or a larger political unit is necessary if that and similar problems are to be dealt with. There is no basis for believing that a multiplicity of communities will think enough alike or spontaneously adopt values compatible enough to operate within a common, accepted framework.

As the number of such complex problems expands, ignoring geographical boundaries, they tend to dwarf in significance the matters dealt with on a community basis. Decentralization becomes an exercise in frustration or impotence. As long as decentralization confers autonomy, some communities can jeopardize the welfare of others through their unconstrained decisions. If decentralized units are constrained, the illusion of autonomy is pierced.

Moreover, in part the challenges to our system arise *because* of the traditions of autonomy which still give significant areas of discretion to private units, at the expense of society as a whole. We have observed the inflationary impact of unconstrained organizational competition. Indeed, behind the decentralist pluralist doctrine lies a neo-Benthamism which is as dubious a philosophy as that accompanying the original utilitarian individualist doctrine. If we are no longer willing to follow Bentham in believing that society is nothing but the sum of its individuals, can we with any more reason assert that it is simply the sum of its organizations or its local communities?

We have been examining in this chapter the principal strategies—incrementalism and decentralization—with which the challenges being raised to present social values might be met while still preserving the essence of those values. It would appear that decentralization by itself is an inadequate reliance. At best it serves as a supplement or component of incrementalism. And incrementalism constitutes an effective strategy only if one believes that the challenges confronted are not engendered by the system itself with its supporting values, as necessary consequences of its functioning. If that belief is not justified, if the challenges are generated by the design of the system itself, incremental reforms will at best postpone a harsher denouement; they may also exacerbate it by that postponement.

13

<hr>

Can Social Values
Be Changed?

IF PRESENT social values cannot be preserved, can they be changed? In asking this question, we are in effect asking whether there are any thruster groups on the horizon ready to confront as opportunities the changed circumstances which challenge existing values.

In the preceding chapter we noted the belief of some decentralists that the rise of small, autonomous communities might constitute a spearhead of change. It was argued there that such a communitarian movement (if indeed it can be called a movement) did not qualify as a thruster. Aside from the question of whether significant autonomy is ever possible in the contemporary world, those emphasizing home rule presumably are not power seekers beyond their own community. Like Gandhi and his philosophy of passive resistance, they can potentially dissolve a larger social system without replacing it. They could at best create a condition which other, more power-oriented groups could exploit. There are several candidates for that role.

One of these consists of a class of managers, both in business and government, to whom we shall apply the designation of techno-centralists. These are individuals who believe that social objectives can best be achieved through the application of scientifically based techniques. The knowledge available for use is greater than the knowledge actually being used. Social ills emerge and remain because politicians, pandering to an emotional public, are more concerned with votes than solutions. Organizational practices and philosophical principles suited to an earlier, more primitive period have lingered on when they should be displaced by more modern techniques supported by an appropriate philosophy.

In particular, the piecemeal (incremental) approach should be abandoned in favor of systems solutions. Instead of viewing society as a field for exploitation by competitive interests, it should be regarded as an intricate mechanism whose parts interact functionally to achieve results which are clearly specified. What people viewed in the simpler past as a discrete individuated unit or institution—a business firm (and business firms generally), a school (and the educational system), a hospital (and the health services as a whole), each of these developed, led, and nourished by its own set of functionaries—can effectively perform a *social* role only if it is recognized as a functional part of a larger system. Each unit has a function which can only be defined in terms of the system's overall performance, and the efficiency of its functioning can only be measured in terms of its contribution to that overall result. To get the results we want, the system must be designed to achieve them. The concepts of efficiency which have led to the successful functioning of our large corporations, all of whose subunits must justify their existence in terms of their contribution to the corporation, should now be extended to society as a whole. Society becomes the corporation writ large, its institutions become the subunits of that larger system, social responsibility gets built into the institutional specifications.

The ones best equipped to carry out this social redesign are scientifically trained managers of large organizations, especially corporations. In the latter, the political element has already been reduced, managerial control is less constrained by popularity polls, and the hierarchic organization facilitates reform and encourages compliance. At the same time, the economic orientation stresses inducement

rather than coercion in securing results—Skinner's positive reinforcement. But business in the United States has always been a
private affair. To achieve *system* coherence, business and government must move towards a *coordinated* functioning. The vision is
spelled out by Simon Ramo, vice chairman of the TRW Corporation:
"Our hybrid economy, part free enterprise and part governmentally
controlled, will take on a new form constituting a virtual Social-Industrial Complex by 1990." [1]

Ramo has been forthright about the institutional and attitudinal
changes which will be necessary. "To create the new pattern of
private-government cooperation, some of us must get over the
hangup that insists government is already too involved in the planning of change." Others must abandon the stereotype that "private
business" means "selfish interest" and that hence only government
can be entrusted with society's welfare. "In providing for defense of
the nation we went beyond consumer-free-enterprise organizational
concepts. A combine of government, industry, and science and technology was formed and it met the nation's requirements for weapons
systems. Similarly, a new combine will be needed to utilize our basic
capabilities to meet the new public demand for social-engineering
projects." The older, simplistic, competitive thinking which led to
such now outdated social devices as antitrust legislation and restrictive regulation must give way to new organizational concepts, involving "social-technological-economic interfaces, much planning,
and considerable control. We must abandon the idea that to articulate
objectives and study alternative plans [for achieving them] is to em-
bark on a one-way road to a complete state control of the economy
and the life pattern. Instead, it may be that to have freedom where it
counts will require planning for freedom."

Few business leaders have been as explicit as Ramo in outlining a
techno-centralist system, but a number have embraced compatible
views. Thomas J. Watson, Jr., when chairman of IBM, told the
Bond Club of New York that "the complexity of our modern economy demands national goal setting and planning [which] should be
costed and readjusted on an integrated basis just as a larger industrial

enterprise sets and controls its goals.'' [2] This is a far less sweeping or visionary conception than Ramo's, but it fits within that framework. More significant is the conclusion of the Research and Policy Committee (consisting of fifty businessmen and a sprinkling of educators with business backgrounds) of the Committee for Economic Development:

> The converging of two trends—the business thrust into social fields, and government's increasing use of market incentives to induce even greater business involvement—is gradually bringing these two powerful institutions into a constructive partnership for accelerating social progress. This emerging partnership is more than a contractual relationship between a buyer and seller of services. Fundamentally, it offers a new means for developing the innate capabilities of a political democracy and a private enterprise economy into *a new politico-economic system* capable of managing social and technological change in the interest of a better social order. [3]

Despite the strictures of some anti-business reformers, it would be a mistake to view the advocacy of techno-centralism as a conspiracy of big business to exploit society in its own interest. Too many corporate leaders are vehemently opposed to national planning and supportive of present institutions and values for that to be true. T. M. Murphy, chairman of General Motors, would confine governmental intervention to ''situations where one person's unrestricted freedom can seriously inhibit the rights of others,'' of which the number is ''far more limited than government planners commonly assume.'' [4] Most business leaders would agree with Murphy. There is, I think, an uncertain division within business between traditional free-enterprisers and the techno-centralists, and the latter should be considered not spokesmen for business generally but, rather, a thruster group inside business—radical thinkers who would seize on changed circumstances to further a new conception of American society in which they would play an enlarged role. If or as they succeed, one would expect a number of now fence-sitting business leaders to join with them, success creating its own following. One would also anticipate, however, numbers of business leaders who would continue in vigorous opposition.

It would be a mistake, too, to attribute to the techno-centralists a fascist philosophy. The label is pejorative and not descriptive. Their thinking comes much closer to the "scientific" psychological prescriptions of B. F. Skinner. Eschewing the aversive controls to which GM's Murphy clings, they see positive reinforcement —chiefly pecuniary—as the means of inducing voluntary compliance with socially desirable results. Thus the CED's Policy Committee states: "The incentive for profit is the only practicable way of unleashing the power and dynamism of private enterprise on a scale that will be effective in generating social progress." Thus the comments of the late Eli Goldston, president of Eastern Gas and Fuel Associates: "Today's highly professional manager, eyes focused on profit performance, operating with excellent controls and within strict rules in the glare of a public scoreboard, needing growth opportunities, and not limited by conventional business boundaries, may be the most promising recruit for solution of the crises in our public service." [5]

Nor does this systems approach—for all its emphasis on scientific technology and social engineering—require thinking of individuals as impersonal atoms in a social organism. Rather, again like Skinner, the new electronic technology would make possible a more direct participation of individuals in both private and public decisions, by registering their preferences and dislikes. They would be fed full information concerning alternatives and costs and benefits. Ramo envisions the possibilities for the citizen as consumer: "A proposal to produce something by a manufacturer could be immediately considered by potential purchasers. . . . We could step to our consoles and push the right buttons to make our commitment." The same possibilities are present for major public decisions. "A national network of computers, communication gear, electronic memory, and information input and output consoles" can permit people "to choose a preference from a group of well-presented alternatives.

153

The public in 1990 could tune in on the issues and take part by expressing its reactions electronically in two-way communication—'instant democracy.' '' Ramo may be somewhat naive in believing that the information flows will be neutral, but the *intent* is clearly benign.

There is a long history of intellectual support for a technocentralist system. From St. Simon and Comte, in rationalist nineteenth-century France, the idea germinated in American minds to a point where John W. Draper, scientist and historian, could write in the immediate post-Civil War period, "All animated nature displays a progress to the domination of a central intelligence. . . . Centralization is an inevitable issue in the life of nations." [6]

In the early twentieth century, Thorstein Veblen in *The Engineers and the Price System* argued that "the material welfare of all the advanced peoples rests in the hands of these technicians, if they will . . . constitute themselves the self-directing General Staff of the country's industry." [7] Charles Steinmetz, probably best known as the founder of General Electric's research and development program but also an educator, writer, socialist politician and public official in two socialist administrations in Schenectady, was one of the most vigorous early exponents of a "new epoch." In his view, individualism would be replaced by a cooperative society, and competition would give way to a national "organism" patterned on the model of the corporation. Science and planning, in the interests of social progress, would obviate the need for traditional politics. [8]

The Great Depression spawned a number of proposals for effectuating Steinmetz's vision, perhaps the best known being that of the Technocracy movement. At the beginning of World War II, James Burnham set out the lineaments of the "Managerial Revolution." More recently, Herbert Simon has effectively analyzed the "new science of management decision," in which—with accumulating knowledge—unprogrammed decisions yield to programming, and management decisions become more centralized, rationalized, and depersonalized, coordinating the parts of the corporation more efficiently in the solution of its problems. [9] Though Simon does not himself make the application, the logic of his analysis would carry beyond the corporation to society as a whole, with the corporation becoming the subsystem of the larger social system. The line of intellectual support for the techno-centralist position continues into the present and includes many respected scientists, some less specific than others in their advocacy of such a system but generating the materials and conclusions supportive of those who do advocate it.

One could, perhaps, maintain that a systems approach will simply evolve within our present institutional and value structure, and there is no doubt that our present structure will accommodate a good deal more of the systems philosophy. To limit its effective spread to what *can* be accommodated is, however, to emasculate it. A systems-planning approach, to achieve its potential and its intent, must start with a clearly defined purpose, and a central administration which coordinates the institutions of the country to achieve the social purpose. This cannot readily be done with the existing institutions. Techno-centralists emerge as a genuine thruster group, in the face of social problems which the present system cannot solve. They come with a new sense of social organization and with their own set of values.

And what are those values? Clearly, they include a more embracing hierarchical form of control, however much relying on positive reinforcements to create the illusion of voluntarism. A corporate social system would seek its defined objectives with greater enforced efficiency, with plans and budgets and performance reviews. The defined objectives—the focal value—would almost certainly remain materialistic: the scientific-technical orientation would guarantee that. They may include a larger component of public consumption (space probes, transportation systems) and environmental programs (technology policing itself), but a utilitarian philosophy would control. The distributive value would continue to stress reward for ability and achievement under conditions of equal opportunity (meritocracy), but probably within some system of administered incomes and prices (planned equity). The disruptive effects of inflation would not be compatible with programmed performance. Inequalities in distribution would thus persist, but with greater attention to their justification by objective criteria.

In the face of intensified challenges to present values, such a social vision might well draw a popular following. Its most vigorous opponents could be expected to be the small business and professional class—the petit bourgeoisie—that would be swallowed up in a bureaucracy beyond its control. But for wage-earners and (ultimately, though reluctantly) for higher management the prospect of a more orderly set of social relations promising benefits no less than they now receive might be very appealing. Techno-centralist thrusters might well win a following, might induce other groups to identify with them, and might succeed in identifying themselves with the nation's welfare and progress.

One criticism which almost certainly would be directed to a technocratic system would be that it offered private profit for social performance. Even within a system of administered prices, profit would constitute the principal positive reinforcer of socially desirable behavior. For it to be effective, it would have to accrue to those who made the responsible decisions, the managers. Under the circumstances, those most inclined to egalitarian principles might well raise the question of why some elite class should reap special reward only for performing the functional requirements of its social role.

On this distributive issue, socialism is doctrinally emphatic. It not only embraces equal opportunity but abjures gross inequality of condition. Socialist practice is less pure than its preachment, to be sure, and significant income differences have emerged in all socialist societies, in some more than in others. Nevertheless, on balance, socialism can claim a pragmatic compromise in modifying inequality. Can we then expect that an American socialist movement might emerge as a thruster group competing with the techno-centralists, offering the same system solutions to the challenges facing the country but incorporating the private corporations into a public system? Profit from what are clearly social institutions could be diverted to the public treasury, managers could be made public servants whose rewards would be commensurate with, and not more than, those accorded public officials already running government departments and agencies.

The overriding reason why a socialist challenge is unlikely in the United States is that it lacks an organized base. There is not, as there has been and is in European countries, a labor movement (or a wing of it) dedicated to its victory. The large suburban middle-class population would vigorously resist any threat to the legitimacy of private property. If socialism emerged in the United States it would have to do so as a spontaneous populist program, championed by a political party captained by professional politicians skilled in demagoguery. Its success would require either a degree of widespread disillusionment and despair sufficient to induce the many with a stake in the present system to believe that that stake could be better preserved under a different system, or a social bankruptcy so profound as to wipe out all stakes and necessitate a fresh start. The possibility of such a populist-socialist thruster movement is not to be dismissed out of hand, but it seems less likely to achieve acceptance than the techno-centralist solution.

Is it possible that a thruster group in American society might have its origins on the international scene? A change in the world order could have its impact on the United States. Such a change might arise from a number of sources, and it is unnecessary for our purposes to explore all the possibilities. It is enough to recognize that any foreign threat would increase the importance of the American military establishment, and a continuing serious threat might propel it into the stance of a thruster group, asserting its own values as essential to the security of the nation. Is this a realistic possibility?

The role which distinguishes the military from other social institutions is its command over force in the advancement and protection of national interests and honor. In the words of one observer, "Basically, the military is an isolated, traditionalist society, immersed in an almost monastic sense of duty." [10]

In recent years the isolation from the rest of society has been much reduced. Military officers have been more deeply involved in foreign affairs, especially if the quasi-military Central Intelligence Agency is included. Through weapons contracting the military has established close operational linkages with American business. Many of its retired officers now serve with major corporations, and there has been a reverse flow of industry men to Pentagon positions. Universities are dependent on Department of Defense grants for the financial support of research, especially in the sciences. Army surveillance machinery has been enlisted by the federal government to prevent suspected subversion or radical agitation. Despite this more activist stance of the modern military, the sense of a mission limited to the nation's protection—a professional sense of duty—remains focal for it.

The American constitutional value has traditionally stressed the subordination of the military's coercive force to civilian rule. That principle has been so well ingrained in the military leadership that it may be safely assumed that only a major upheaval *within* the military would dislodge it. An occasional general—a Douglas MacArthur—may challenge the rule, but he is the exception. There is no military faction chafing at civilian restraint as a principle, however embittered some officers may be at being kept "on a leash" during specific field operations. Any speculation on the rise of the military as a thruster group in the United States must realistically begin by ruling out a coup.

But the changing objective conditions confronting American society might well promote greater public reliance on the military role. The United States now lives in a world largely hostile (if still sometimes deferential) to it. The challenges which it faces extend from expropriation of its nationals' investments (now accepted as a matter of course) to uninhibited guerrilla attacks on its citizens, agents, and commercial carriers; from cancellation of leases of military installations to overt or covert threats of war. America's defense needs grow greater, and the military becomes more strategic in its foreign policy.

But that is only half the story. External threats are matched by internal decay. The source is the cities, as we have already noted, and the cause is chiefly the racial confrontation which they spawn. The Kerner Commission's warning of the growing irreconcilability of two societies, one black and urban, the other white and suburban, has gone largely unheeded. There may be no reasonable basis for expecting anything but increases in lawlessness, declining civilities and amenities with consequent flight to the suburbs by those who can afford it; an erosion of urban economic activity concomitant with a rise in urban poverty; and fiscal inadequacy and perhaps even political bankruptcy, brought on by the incapability of some local governments to preserve not only the peace but necessary civic functions.

If these forbidding prospects should materialize, the federal government could not remain aloof. But the rehabilitation of the cities would require more than a flow of public funds. It would require economic, political, and social redevelopment, which, since it is beyond the demonstrated capacity of local officials, would have to be carried out by a trustee government—in effect, an imposed government. This would necessarily involve access to a responsible and disciplined police force—"independent of the town population and able to repress its excesses," as Tocqueville said with his extraordinary prescience—and not on an ad hoc or temporary basis but as a longer lasting federal instrument. What alternative would there be to some form of military government in the major cities?

Whether even the military could reclaim the cities to a viable order would depend on their finding support for necessary programs on a national scale. Urban order would not be established simply by putting men in uniforms on the streets. It would call for economic and political programs integrating the urban centers with the rest of the country, instead of leaving them isolated islands. Thus the military would soon enough find that to carry out the mission assigned them would require their becoming more deeply involved in social and economic policy, exercising influence in Congress in these areas just as they have in the more traditional military areas. They could be expected to develop their own economic specialists, capable of arguing the needs for the cities more effectively than the politically fragmented and shorter-term city mayors under present political arrangements.

In short, we would find the military emerging as a genuine thruster group not because it lusts for power but because changing objective conditions would have provided a richer field of opportunities for the exercise of its role. Both on the international and domestic fronts, events would give greater weight to its monopoly of force as an instrument for national redemption and salvation. The events in question would not have been created by the military as the vehicle for their rise to greater power. Those events would nonetheless constitute the opportunities on which the military would seize—out of a sense of its mission and associated values—to carry through its vision of the form of society appropriate to the circumstances. It would impress on the society those values to which it, as a functional group, is deeply committed. The easy identification of the military's own group values with national values which we earlier observed to be characteristic of a thruster group would apply here. The confusion of group values and group interests, with protection of the latter seen as necessary to advancement of the former, could likewise be expected.

A military thruster group would scarcely set itself against the old business dominants, attempting to displace them. It would be much more likely that a working alliance would be effected, just as between military and church in an earlier day. The military-industrial complex, which has been so often regarded as a kind of sinister conspiracy for the furtherance of special interests, would emerge as a welcomed leadership class, drawing to itself other allies and supporters such as the scientists and technologists. Larger numbers of "little thrusters" and opportunists, of adaptables and tolerants, of admirers of power and success would form a base of support.

And what would be the values affirmed by the new leadership class? In the area of focal values, there would be a movement away from preoccupation with private consumption toward a doctrine of austerity for the benefit and rehabilitation of the nation as a whole. Such a doctrine would permit a diversion of production to military preparedness, on the one hand, and to the vast domestic reconstruction that is needed (in housing, transportation, and urban redevelopment) on the other hand. This shift of the focal value from private to public needs could be expected to appeal to idealists and intellectuals who on their own would have little prospect of asserting alternative values.

In the area of constitutional values, the shift would be predictably toward the assertion of the hierarchical forms of control on which military organization depends. Military government in the major cities would be almost certain to undermine present constitutional values of individual autonomy as embodied in the Bill of Rights, but their loss might be accepted philosophically by a population which sees that as necessary for the achievement of the new focal value.

In the area of distributive values, one might anticipate a reinforced emphasis on rank and privilege, but a greater equality of condition *within* the ranks. It is entirely compatible with such an outlook that racial equality would be more nearly enforced, as it has already been within the military establishment.

It is worth recalling that the military life has not been without its advocates in the United States, even among intellectuals. The significant consideration has always been the cause it serves. Even Emerson, who in the heat of Civil War enthusiasm accepted an appointment as official visitor to West Point, came away with a glow of respect for the emphasis on discipline and order, and a sudden insight that Lycurgus's Sparta had much to recommend it. Herman Melville, disillusioned by 1865, was led to believe that America had outgrown her earlier dreams and could best be served by a strong authority restraining its masses. Theodore Roosevelt exalted the strenuous life exemplified by the man of arms. Edward Bellamy's utopian novel, *Looking Backward,* set in the year 2000, envisioned a military-like organization of industry with workers animated by duty, service, and patriotism. William James spoke with respect of the ideals inculcated by military service, and looked for a moral *equivalent* of war. (Nor is it without interest that James's plea has surfaced so repeatedly in recent years.) There is some historical basis for surmising, then, that an enlarged role for the military, directed to a cause with which idealists and realists alike might identify—particularly in its domestic function—might enlist substantial popular support.[11]

Of the three potential thruster groups we have considered, the corporate techno-centralists or a military leadership seem more likely than a socialist movement. Nor need these two candidates for national influence oppose each other. There would be no insuperable obstacle to their collaboration.

Nevertheless, I do not expect that it will be one of these two, or even these two in harness, which will offer the most appealing program for coping with present and prospective challenges. The military solution would require so fundamental a change in our constitutional values—generals succeeding generals, without popular election?—that it is hard to envision except as a temporary expedient in time of crisis. (Even Rome, for all its skill in government, found no solution to the problem of maintaining under civil authority a military class which in fact had been raised to power.) The techno-centralist approach is too much concerned with hardware. Like its scientific-management predecessors, this view seems to advocate either that political decisions are unreliable and should be replaced by more rationalized procedures, or that instant popular decisions—the computer substituting for the inefficient pollster—satisfy any requirements of public political involvement. Stressing efficiency of *system* performance, the functional role of people as parts, it escalates the payoff in goods and results for routine *individual* performance (like employee, like citizen). Emphasizing that its enlistment in social objectives is to be achieved through profit incentives, it arouses suspicion that the corporation is simply co-opting government for its own ends.

To identify weaknesses in the position of these two potential thruster groups is not, however, to disparage their possible contributions. I cannot help but believe that the military will play a more significant domestic role in the future than it has in the past, but that role will, I think, continue to serve subordinate ends specified by civil authority. Force is likely to play a more important part in the preservation of civic order, and the relationship of the federal government to the cities is likely to increase in importance. The two trends—if such they are—suggest a larger peacetime contribution of the military but not a dominant national position.

Can Social Values Be Changed?

The techno-centralists are of greater interest to our present inquiry. However tentative the probings of the Committee for Economic Development and other business leaders, some of their number show an appropriate recognition that prevailing values may excessively constrain the achievement of social welfare. There is no reason to believe that those who are moving in this direction are so wedded to technological solutions of a systems nature that they would eschew alternative ways of redefining the corporate role. What seems evident is that among corporate leaders there is emerging a small number who are not only willing to entertain the prospect—indeed, the necessity—of social change, but who are also beginning to ask themselves whether the corporation may not be the best instrument for bringing that change about. Not the corporation as it functions today, since conditions are outmoding that, but the corporation functioning in a different way, to meet the challenges of the times. Let us explore further that possibility.

14

Social Entrepreneurship

EVEN IF economic growth does not come up against inexorable limits, its pursuit can no longer function as our chief social goal, in the sense of "the more the better." Already we are conditioning ourselves to constraints on economic growth in piecemeal fashion. We may attempt to soften the impact, even disguise it, by refashioning our statistical measures of national income to include such things as the unpaid services of housewives (even the value of leisure time has been suggested, and *Lysistrata* suggests another daring possibility), but the underlying circumstances are not thereby altered.

Individual autonomy is no longer as possible as in a simpler society. The orderly functioning of the social system, on which each individual depends for his own welfare, requires an increasingly centralized authority, a coordinating role backed by coercive power, accepted by—not imposed on—the public out of necessity.

Initial distribution of rewards through organizational competition, and an illusory redistributive egalitarianism through government deficit spending, both lead to rates of inflation and unemployment which are socially unacceptable.

These major challenges to contemporary American values reflect causal changes in the objective conditions confronting us. They are the basis for that deepening pessimism of which we took note at the outset of this inquiry. But if such changes are indeed occurring, as I believe they are, we confront them as *facts* to be dealt with. Since they cannot be wished away, they become, inevitably, the *basis* for *some* system capable of building on them. As the physicist Werner Heisenberg has said with reference to scientific change, "Our choice seems to be restricted to the decision *whether or not we want to participate* in a development that takes place in our time, with or without our efforts and contributions." [1]

The force of this position as it applies to the corporation seems to have penetrated the thinking of some business leaders. If the corporation is to play as large a role in the future as it has in the past it will have to be a different corporation. But having recognized this need, how bring about the result?

No single corporation, however imaginative its management, can escape from the web of institutional rules which it (and its predecessors) has helped to weave and maintain. The values which it has supported—individualistic competition in particular—preclude its taking independent initiative and forbid, too, its collaborating on change with other corporations. Trapped by its own values, it can only compete vigorously to make as much of a profit as it can, for the benefit of its own constituents, by promoting the greater consumption of its output—the very activities which are now called into question.

Any initiative to change significantly the character of the corporation must first be directed at changing the institutional rules within which the corporation functions. This is something which requires governmental action. The initiative for change may come from corporate leaders, but it will have to be directed externally rather than channeled internally. This invokes the contingency which the CED report on corporate responsibility foresaw, but encompasses a larger field of reform. If competition restrained the corporation from undertaking desirable social activity, like pollution abatement, because such activity would put the corporation at a competitive disadvantage, the CED (or at least its policy committee) believed that corporate managements should themselves propose and support government regulations binding on all. Moreover, the CED was prepared to accept new, hybrid types of public-private corporations if these were needed to combine the best attributes of government and business.

As progressive and commendable as such recommendations are, they envisage a population of private corporations only slightly different from the present. This is not surprising. More sweeping initiatives are unlikely to emerge from any organized group encompassing a spectrum of opinion. The need for more radical change will, in the first instance, be recognized by a relatively small number of corporate iconoclasts—a genuine thruster group. Their perception of how social changes are making present forms of organization obsolete will prompt proposals for governmental intervention which will be, to put it mildly, unacceptable to most of their fellow business leaders.

Obviously, efforts to reshape the rules governing corporate conduct to meet the challenges of the times, undertaken by a small number of corporate leaders and fought by a larger number, are unlikely to meet with swift success. But if the premise is valid—and the objective circumstances are indeed changing in ways which will make the functioning of corporations as presently structured more difficult, ineffective, and unacceptable—then the prospect for more sweeping reform increases. Who could have foreseen in 1928 the acceptance—by business and public alike—of the radical (if temporary) retreat from individualistic competition embodied in the National Industrial Recovery Act of only a few years later?

In the face of major social changes which render existing institutions inadequate, pressures for reform can be almost irresistible. By laying the groundwork for reform before crisis compels it, the thrusters increase the chances that *their* method of coping with challenge, rather than some other, will be tried. Suggestions, proposals, trial balloons which were earlier attacked for being subversive of existing values will be accorded greater respect with the collapse of those values—and this will occur not because of conspiracy or attack, but because the values will no longer sustain the weight of changing circumstance.

The restructuring of the corporation under a leadership professing different values will elicit support from other groups only if they see their own welfare advanced by identifying with the thrusters. It is too much to expect that tentative proposals for change, such as suggestions for increased business collaboration with government, are likely now to arouse much enthusiasm among other interest groups— labor unions, for example—since they meet with opposition even within the ranks of business itself. The present leaders of other interest groups occupy their positions precisely because they can work effectively with the present business leadership. Their fortunes rise and fall together. But if changing objective conditions reveal more and more clearly the inadequacy of present values and institutions, then the inside business thrusters, offering feasible solutions, will have their supporting counterparts inside other groups. As social change compels institutional change, those counterparts can be expected to rise to more influential roles concomitantly with the rising thrusters. Policies which have been roundly rejected by organized business and labor alike—price and wage controls, for example—may be better received by new leaders rising within both sectors, who attempt to cope with challenges rather than deny their existence.

And what will be the shape of the restructured corporation within a changing society? The design can hardly be pulled off the shelf, a systems solution complete in all its details. It will have to be developed in the same way that most institutional change occurs, bit by bit but in a fresh direction. The new structure will be validated not by the internal logic of its design but by its capacity to organize social relationships which satisfy the needs of the times.

The general nature of the value and institutional changes which now seem appropriate can perhaps be suggested without advancing a grand design or attempting unwarranted detail. We can identify some of the likely ingredients without claiming them to be necessary.

The first requirement would seem to be a clearer definition of social objectives and their incorporation in a national plan. The scarcity condition underlies all economic and most social decisions, necessitating the allocation of resources to some purposes rather than others. We have left choice largely to the private sector, and the result has been social decay. For some years the Joint Economic Committee of Congress, joined in 1970 by a Republican president, has been urging the desirability of:

— assessing national needs, collecting information and developing forecasts, for the purpose of defining national goals and objectives, and

— coordinating the establishment of national priorities for the allocation of available resources.[2]

The CED's policy committee, in its report on corporate responsibilities, envisioned that the government's enlarged involvement might include

— a major share of responsibility for [corporate] financing through appropriations, public borrowing, loan guarantees, and

— over-all planning so that the corporation's activities fit sensibly into the total environmental system in which it operates.[3]

The kind of planning operation which is most frequently proposed follows the French model. It is based on an estimate of available resources, a specification of principal socio-economic objectives by the National Assembly, and an "indication" worked out in a number of sectoral commissions manned by government, business, and labor representatives of what would be the desirable participation of each sector in the overall plan. The participation is not compelled but induced by incentives, chiefly involving access to capital funds. The social objectives can be pursued with varying degrees of firmness, depending on their relative importance. Large areas of economic activity can be left to private decision, affected only in terms of their overall magnitudes—so much of the national output indicated for household electrical appliances, for example, or even some larger category, without any more detailed specification. The intent is to insure that the most important social needs are met while leaving other choices open to individuals. The functioning of the corporation remains as discretionary as possible, consonant only with the achievement of those social objectives considered too vital to leave to chance.

One of the crucial questions is how investment funds are to be allocated to insure that social priorities are realized. If the CED assigns to government a larger role in raising capital funds, it must necessarily assign government a larger role in allocating them. One way would be to make funds available to all firms meeting a competitive structure of interest rates—all firms which can pay the rates that "clear" the capital market are given their share. This may be an appropriate method when all production is treated alike as long as it meets the market test, but it will scarcely do when social objectives are to be given priority. Selective credit availability seems necessary, both with respect to access and terms, if capital is to be steered to certain preferred uses before being made more generally available.

No contemporary society can do without some form of full-employment program. The employment offered should, however, be recognized as contributing to society's wants as much as to the worker's need for income. Make-work is both demeaning and wasteful. The formula of "government as employer of last resort" makes government into the marginal employer, and the worker a marginal contributor. The line between the usefulness of private and public employment is a fallacious one, or at least should be. The employment of all able workers on useful projects, and not only the allocation of claims to income, should be the objective. It could presumably be accomplished by government contracts with private business, or—less desirably—by government itself assuming a production (not just employing) role, for whatever purposes are needed or wanted.

Unquestionably the most difficult problem is the distributional one. With large-scale corporate and labor organization, it is hardly to be expected that national income will continue to be allocated on the basis of organizational competition, allowing those who occupy the most strategic positions, or who can mobilize the most commanding bargaining power, to capture superior rewards for themselves. In an "administrative letter" to its members in 1967, the four top officials of the United Automobile Workers (including Walter Reuther, then president, and Leonard Woodcock, present president) called for wage equity in relation to other forms of income, but it asked also for greater equity *among* wage earners. "The wide disparity in wages among workers for the same employer, in the same industry, in the same location obviously calls for national direction from within the labor movement in the form of a basic incomes policy that would more equitably distribute the wealth of the nation among the workers who produce that wealth."

The question then is how to resolve the problem of distributional equity among all income receivers, from whatever source income is derived, including of course the thorny issue of relative wage rates and earnings among workers, organized and unorganized alike. It seems obvious that no formula is to be found which will satisfy everyone, but it seems equally obvious that some approach to a more acceptable solution is necessary. It will, I suspect, involve setting not only social minimum incomes, about which much has been said in recent years, but also social maximums. Some restraint on the exercise of socially strategic position for individual enrichment will probably have to be set, applying to labor unions and corporate executives alike.

Compliance with wage and salary limitations has always been spotty when attempted in emergency situations in the past. The problem of how to deal with a labor strike called by a strategic union to enforce a wage demand beyond the permissible increase has been a particularly tricky one. That is not to say it is insoluble, however. Once the *need* is accepted, the mechanism can be found. Possibly it may lie in tax measures. The amount by which any wage or salary increase exceeded the permissible limit could be disallowed as a tax-deductible cost and added to profit and taxed as such. It could also be recaptured from the individual receiving it, added to his tax deductions at the source and collected by his employer. Faced with such an enforceable provision, labor unions would find intransigence unrewarding and corporate executives might be less disposed to award themselves bonuses.

Social Entrepreneurship

A limitation on wages and salaries would not be equitable unless accompanied by a limitation on profits and a restraint on prices. At the same time, if one objective is to keep governmental oversight to a minimum, it would be desirable to avoid a system of surveillance over the incredibly intricate network of prices, avoiding rules or guidelines which attempt to take into account changes in productivity, effects of cost changes, the relevance of discounts or allowances, changes in the quality of products, and other such complicating considerations. One alternative which would act as control not only over prices but over profits would be to set a maximum allowable rate of return on investment. Anything above that amount would be fully taxed away. The maximum rate would become, in effect, every company's target rate of return. To discourage registering on prices the effect of a higher achieved rate of return, a penalty might be imposed if a firm's return on investment exceeded the allowable maximum by some specified margin.

Under this approach a company would retain discretion in price setting, subject to the overall constraint that, in the aggregate, the prices of its products would not yield a revenue greater than the allowable maximum return. A company's justification for pricing one product higher, another lower, would be of no interest to any federal price regulator, since prices would not in fact be regulated. The government's only interest would be in insuring that whatever price actions a company took did not add up to an excess rate of profit.

A maximum allowable rate of return on investment would dilute somewhat the present emphasis on competition. We have been brought up believing that somehow individual competition is synonomous with social good: Adam Smith still lives on. But as businessmen themselves have often had occasion to realize, competition can be excessive and destructive. This is likely to be even truer in the future than in the past, if we encounter resource and environmental limits to economic growth. A maximum allowable return on investment would curb somewhat the appetite for maximum growth and might even induce producers to concentrate more attention on improving the quality of their output, further conserving resources.

Distribution of a corporation's allowable earnings could be made subject to certain requirements. It might, for example, be divided into four components. Some percentage might first be diverted to the public treasury (a profits tax). Another specified percentage might be compulsorily distributed as dividends, the amount perhaps only slightly higher than that obtained from a secure bond. A third portion might be made available for discretionary reinvestment, which, when invested, would become part of the investment base on which the maximum allowable rate of return would be computed. If considered desirable for purposes of smoothing the aggregate level of output, the government might—in the Swedish fashion—be empowered to require the temporary impounding of some or all of those reinvestable funds in a special investment account, held in the firm's name and released for its use as economic conditions warranted.

Finally, some portion of the firm's earnings would be earmarked for social, non-profit-making purposes of its own devising—whether pollution controls beyond those required by law, or educational programs in which it would participate, or community-improvement projects, or cultural affairs. It might even use such funds to improve the quality of its own work environment, with some necessary safeguards against fraud and with the proviso that such expenditures could not be added to the investment base on which the rate of return was computed. The intent behind this provision would be to encourage a company to pay greater attention to its social environment, and to use its entrepreneurial skills in improving the quality of that environment. In a limited way, it—and all business firms in the aggregate—would be contributing to the gradual broadening of the focal value beyond the present fixation on consumption.

Such a new corporate role might be expected to appeal to those business leaders who have already averred that business must offer the people who run it greater challenges than production quotas and profit. Those executives who have for years argued that business must serve multiple constituencies have obviously felt constrained by a simple property nexus, as though the holders of its shares were truly its owners, and managers responsible only to them for its policies.

The notion of multiple corporate goals is indeed not vastly different from the concept of the social audit, which a number of business leaders have already embraced. The social audit, in its various versions, ultimately comes down to an evaluation of how the company, in the course of carrying out its economic functions, has affected society on a number of fronts. The social audit is, in effect, a report of the outcome of the company's pursuit of multiple goals. Under a new corporate structure the freedom to pursue those goals would be given greater reality by mandating the use of some portion of earnings for their achievement. Competition among firms, weakened in some measure on the production front by a limitation on profit seeking, might be encouraged on other fronts, in the form of the quality of profit spending.

Indeed, even without extending our vision beyond the actual production process itself, it is arguable that, for example, an automobile industry that is concerned almost solely with how many cars it can pump onto the roads, at maximum profit, no longer meets minimum social expectations. Arguably, we should expect the automobile industry to produce high-quality, long-lasting, low-priced vehicles, as near to non-polluting as possible, safe, dependable, easily and cheaply repaired, and produced under conditions more satisfying to and controllable by the workers who make them. It should be an industry whose concern is not only production but the social effects of that production.

Perhaps some portion of these desired results could be assured by government regulation over the corporation as presently constituted—regulations imposing safety and pollution constraints, for example. But that seems scarcely adequate to meet challenges erupting on other fronts as well, notably the way corporate power (and the organized union power which it begets) affects the distribution of income and the use of resources, including our human resources. A corporation capable of meeting the more complex demands of the future will probably have to be reconstituted so that the initiative and drive for a broader range of activities comes from *within*. Heaping limitations on its present more narrowly channeled motivation neither serves social needs adequately nor reaps the full potential benefit of its energies, which are constrained by regulation rather than released by inducement.

In seeking to unleash entrepreneurial energies for social betterment, it seems probable that present inhibitions on corporate collaboration should be largely removed. The muting of our present emphasis on competition is only one side of the coin. The other side is an encouragement of cooperation. The intent is to preserve organizational autonomy to the fullest extent consonant with social benefit, without precluding joint participation and voluntary agreement in the exercise of that autonomy. With appropriate inducements, joint action need not be conspiracy to benefit at public expense.

We are understandably suspicious of the consequences of business collaboration in a society which stresses competition as the chief principle of distribution. What other purpose could collaboration serve but to improve the competitive position of the collaborators? If, however, material rewards for individual performance, while still accruing, have some upper limit, and if entrepreneurial aspirations can be satisfied through public service as well as private advantage (an ancient and honorable belief), then collaboration—if it occurs— is more likely to be undertaken for social benefit than for private gain. Institutional relations will have been restructured to induce this result. Or have we become so cynical as to doubt that discretionary behavior can indeed be channeled in this direction?

If social objectives have been set within the framework of a national plan which specifies only the most pressing requirements, leaving a large field for autonomous decision, and if the corporation has been partially released from present competitive constraints and induced to use its autonomy in the pursuit of a broader conception of the social welfare, we will be going far towards meeting the challenges to our present values. To achieve that result we will still rely—there is likely to be no better reliance—on the private corporation, but a corporation which is a different species from the present form. The end objective of the social system, of which the corporation is the prime instrument, will not be an engineering-like, economically efficient, highest level productivity of least input per unit of output, translated (in the case of the corporation) into maximum profit. It will involve, much more, political judgments, in the corporation as well as the government, as to how a variety of objectives can best be satisfied in tandem.

The business leaders who come forward with a program to achieve that result, turning their backs on the present too-narrow conception of corporate interest and purpose, will be seeking to realize the opportunities inherent in our present problems. They will constitute genuine thrusters, inside thrusters, ready to recognize that the corporation as social instrument can be preserved only by making it a different institution from what it is today. They envision the corporation of the future as an institution with whose fresh purpose other groups can in time come to identify their interests, whose success will be broadly viewed as conducive to society's advantage as well as its own, and which, in the process of achieving that success, can perhaps forge a new national identity based on a new set of values. This is a daring, perhaps even an arrogant, ambition, but that is characteristic of thrusters.

Heisenberg, writing again of science, a science which historically involved philosophy, a philosophy which historically involved also political relations, summarizes the forward pull of opportunities implicit in seeming dead ends, even though we still tend to define those opportunities in terms of traditions.

> What is really needed is a change in fundamental concepts. We will have to abandon the philosophy of Democritus and the concept of fundamental elementary particles. And, instead, we will have to accept the concept of fundamental symmetries which is a concept out of the philosophy of Plato.
>
> Just as Copernicus and Galileo abandoned in their method the descriptive science of Aristotle and turned to the structural science of Plato, so we are probably being forced in our concepts to abandon the atomic materialism of Democritus and to turn to the ideas of symmetry in the philosophy of Plato.[4]

To abandon atomic materialism—of social relations, no less than science. To search for symmetry, balance, and new structural relations—in society, no less than in the physical world. The parallels between the scientist's view of the needs of our times and the social analyst's are striking. If, as Heisenberg laconically remarks of science, "We need not invent our problems," the same can also be said of society. They exist. The best response to those problems—after an understandable shock of identification—is not to lament or deny their existence but to run on them as a target. That kind of response is in the very nature of thrusters.

NOTES

Chapter 1

1. Alexis de Tocqueville, *Democracy in America,* ed. Phillips Bradley (New York: Random House, 1945), vol. 1, pp. 409–10.
2. Sheldon S. Wolin, "Prometheus in America," a review of Richard N. Goodwin's *The American Condition, New York Review of Books,* May 2, 1974, p. 10.
3. The theory of formation and change of values which is here much condensed has been developed at length in my previous book, *The Place of Business in America's Future: A Study in Social Values* (New York: Basic Books, 1973).

Chapter 4

1. Alan Simpson, *Puritanism in Old and New England* (Chicago: University of Chicago Press, 1955), p. 58.
2. Quoted in Rebecca Gruver, *American Nationalism: Self-Portrait* (New York: G. P. Putnam's Sons, 1970), p. 77.
3. Michel Chevalier, *Society, Manners, and Politics in the United States,* ed. John William Ward (Ithaca, N.Y.: Cornell University Press, 1961), p. 254.
4. Clement Eaton, *The Leaven of Democracy* (New York: George Braziller, 1963), p. 23.
5. C. Vann Woodward, "Seeing Slavery Whole," a review of Eugene Genovese's *Roll, Jordan, Roll, New York Review,* Oct. 3, 1974, p. 19.
6. Dick Friedman, "The Foot-ball Question," *Yale Alumni Magazine,* November 1974, p. 18.
7. Chester I. Barnard, *The Functions of the Executive* (Cambridge, Mass.: Harvard University Press, 1936), p. 204.
8. William Miller, "American Historians and the Business Elite," *Journal of Economic History* 9 (November 1949), pp. 184–208; idem, "The Recruitment of the American Business Elite," *Quarterly Journal of Economics* 64 (May 1950): 329–37.
9. Moses Rischin, *The American Gospel of Success* (Chicago: Quadrangle Books, 1965), p. 10.
10. Theodore Dreiser, in "Life, Art and America," quoted in *American Realism,* ed. Jane Benardette (New York: Putnam's, 1972), p. 348.

Notes

11. Friedman, "Foot-ball Question," p. 18.

12. H. Stuart Hughes, "They Don't Make Them Like That Any More," a review of *The Autobiographical Notes of Charles Evans Hughes, New York Review,* May 30, 1974, p. 33.

13. Ibid.

14. Quoted in Ray Ginger, *The Age of Excess* (New York: Macmillan, 1965), p. 32.

15. Lincoln Steffens, *The Autobiography of Lincoln Steffens* (New York: Harcourt, Brace and Co., 1931), p. 606.

Chapter 5

1. Charles Morley, ed., *Portrait of America: Letters of Henry Sienkiewicz* (New York: Columbia University Press, 1959), pp. 6, 15, 22.

2. Alexis de Tocqueville, *Democracy in America,* ed. Phillips Bradley (New York: Random House, 1945), vol. 1, p. 53.

3. Chevalier, *Society, Manners, and Politics in The United States,* ed. John William Ward (Ithaca, N.Y.: Cornell University Press, 1961), p. 262.

4. Alan Simpson, *Puritanism in Old and New England* (Chicago: University of Chicago Press, 1955), ch. 3.

5. Cotton Mather, *A Christian at His Calling* (1701), reprinted in Moses Rischin, *The American Gospel of Success* (Chicago: Quadrangle, 1965), pp. 23, 24, 26.

6. Simpson, *Puritanism,* p. 34.

7. Moses Rischin, *American Gospel,* p. 3. (Whitman's *Democratic Vistas* was published in 1871.)

8. Chevalier, *Society, Manners, and Politics,* p. 268.

9. Morley, *Portrait of America,* p. 19.

10. Lloyd G. Reynolds and Joseph Shister, *Job Horizons* (New York: Harper & Bros., 1949).

11. Frank Presbrey, cited by Edward C. Kirkland in *Industry Comes of Age: 1860–1897* (New York: Holt, Rinehart and Winston, 1961), p. 272.

12. *Nation,* 20 (May 20, 1875): 342.

13. Wesley Frank Craven, *The Legend of the Founding Fathers* (Ithaca, N.Y.: Cornell University Press, 1965), p. 147.

14. David M. Potter, *People of Plenty* (Chicago: University of Chicago Press, 1954), pp. 176–77.

15. Ibid., p. 182.

16. Caryl Rivers, "How To Be Spotless, Sexy and Loved," *New York Times,* April 28, 1974.

17. Quoted in Alpheus T. Mason, *Security Through Freedom* (Ithaca, N.Y.: Cornell University Press, 1955), p. 49.

Notes

Chapter 6

1. R. R. Palmer, *The Age of the Democratic Revolution* (Princeton, N.J.: Princeton University Press, 1959), vol. 1, pp. 366, 407, 215.

2. Michel Chevalier, *Society, Manners, and Politics in the United States,* ed. John William Ward (Ithaca, N.Y.: Cornell University Press, 1961), p. 43.

3. Alexis de Tocqueville, *Democracy in America,* ed. Phillips Bradley (New York: Random House, 1945), vol. 1, p. 274.

4. Chevalier, *Society, Manners, and Politics,* pp. 327–29.

5. Paul McNulty, "The Consumer and the Producer," *Yale Review,* 58 (Summer 1969): 537–42.

6. Edward Kirkland, *Industry Comes of Age: 1860–1897* (New York: Holt, Rinehart and Winston, 1961), p. 310.

7. Ibid., p. 312.

8. Quoted in Alpheus T. Mason, *Security Through Freedom* (Ithaca, N.Y.: Cornell University Press, 1955), p. 39.

9. Ibid., p. 51.

10. James Harvey Robinson, *The Mind in the Making* (New York: Harper & Brothers, 1921), p. 202. Robinson continues: "It [business] is defended by the civil government even as the later Roman emperors and the medieval princes protected the Church against attack. Socialists and communists are the Waldensians and Albigensians of our day, heretics to be cast out, suppressed, and deported to Russia, if not directly to hell as of old. The Secret Service seems inclined to play the part of a modern Inquisition, which protects our new religion. Collected in its innumerable files is the evidence in regard to suspected heretics who have dared impugn 'business as usual,' or who have dwelt too lovingly on peace and good will among nations. Books and pamphlets, although no longer burned by the common hangman, are forbidden the mails by somewhat undiscerning officials."

11. Bruce A. Ackerman, "Jerome Frank's Law and the Modern Mind," *Daedalus,* 703 (Winter 1974): 120. Ackerman comments that the Supreme Court's decisions of the 1920s and 1930s "striking down social welfare legislation were hardly an exercise of arbitrary power by five or six men in black robes; indeed, they were deeply rooted in dominant patterns of legal thought. . . . Because of this legal culture, the judges could, without a sense of arbitrariness or impropriety, strike down a minimum–wage law on the ground that it deprived the women of Washington, D.C., of the right to work for less than $16.50 a week."

12. Alpheus T. Mason, *Security Through Freedom,* p. 75.

Chapter 7

1. Russell B. Nye, *This Almost Chosen People* (East Lansing: Michigan State University Press, 1967), pp. 317–18.

Notes

2. Charles Morley, ed., *Portrait of America: Letters of Henry Sienkiewicz* (New York: Columbia University Press, 1959), p. 92.

3. Ibid., p. 98.

4. Michel Chevalier, *Society, Manners, and Politics in the United States,* ed. John William Ward (Ithaca, N.Y.: Cornell University Press, 1961), p. 271.

5. Nye, *This Almost Chosen People,* p. 130.

6. Edward Kirkland, *Industry Comes of Age: 1860–1897* (New York: Holt, Rinehart and Winston, 1961), p. 81. The Union Pacific president, Sidney Dillon, went on to argue the immutability of the competitive principle. "No power can prevent one man or set of men from offering to perform a lawful service at lower rates than another." Dillon obviously did not foresee the fair–pricing legislation which was to be written forty years later.

7. Ibid.

8. Nye, *This Almost Chosen People,* p. 133.

9. John P. Marquand, *Point of No Return* (New York: Bantam, 1956), pp. 161–62.

10. Herbert Hoover, *American Individualism* (New York: Doubleday, Page & Co., 1922), pp. 9–10.

11. Alexis de Tocqueville, *Democracy in America,* ed. Phillips Bradley (New York: Random House, 1945), vol. 1, p. 262.

12. E. Digby Baltzell, *Philadelphia Gentlemen* (New York: Quadrangle Books, 1971), p. 384.

13. Quoted by Edmund Wilson, in *The Bit Between My Teeth* (New York: Farrar, Strauss, and Giroux, 1966), p. 68.

14. William C. Bullitt, *It's Not Done* (New York: Harcourt, Brace and Co., 1926), pp. 307–308; quoted in Baltzell, *Philadelphia Gentlemen,* p. 191.

15. *Yale Alumni Magazine,* April 1974, p. 24.

Chapter 8

1. *Atlantic Monthly,* 232 (September 1973): 84.

2. David Finn, *The Corporate Oligarch* (New York: Simon and Schuster, 1970), p. 87.

3. Edmund Wilson, "An Appeal to Progressives," in *The Shores of Light* (New York: Farrar, Strauss, 1952), p. 527.

4. Gregory Bateson, *Steps to an Ecology of Mind* (New York: Ballantine, 1972), pp. 426–39.

5. Fletcher L. Byrom, "Corporate Policy Applied to a Finite World," mimeographed (speech delivered at the First Biennial Assessment of Alternatives to Growth, The Woodlands, Texas, Oct. 21, 1975), pp. 7, 15.

6. J. Edwin Matz, "Fuels of the Future," *Harvard Business Review,* 53 (Nov.– Dec. 1975): 177.

Notes

Chapter 9

1. Lincoln Steffens, *Autobiography* (New York: Harcourt, 1931) pp. 855–856.

2. John Dos Passos, *The Fourteenth Chronicle: Letters and Diaries of John Dos Passos,* ed. Townsend Ludington (Boston: Gambit, 1973), p. 579. (The quotation comes from a letter to Edmund Wilson, Oct. 29, 1947.)

3. Ibid, pp. 180, 208. (Journal notes of April 20, 1918 and Aug. 30, 1918.)

4. Richard N. Goodwin, *The American Condition* (New York: Doubleday, 1974).

5. Herbert Marcuse, *Eros and Civilization* (New York: Random House, Vintage Books, 1955), p. 89.

6. Eric Hoffer, "What We Have Lost," *New York Times Magazine,* Oct. 20, 1974, p. 110.

7. Robert Penn Warren, "Bearers of Bad Tidings: Writers and the American Dream," *New York Review,* March 20, 1975, p. 17.

8. Philip M. Hauser, "Mobilizing for a Just Society," mimeographed (Presidential address at the National Conference of Social Welfare, Annual Forum, Cincinnati, Ohio, May 19, 1974), passim.

9. B. F. Skinner, *Beyond Freedom and Dignity* (New York: Bantam, 1972), pp. 196–97.

10. Ibid., pp. 172, 174.

11. Ibid., pp. 167, 169.

12. B. F. Skinner, *Walden II* (New York: Macmillan, 1948), p. 220. (The statement is made by the chief architect of Skinner's utopian society, in this fictional work.)

13. Isaiah Berlin, "The Question of Machiavelli," *The New York Review,* Nov. 4, 1971, pp. 20–32.

Chapter 10

1. Lee Rainwater, *What Money Buys* (New York: Basic Books, 1974), pp. 174–5.

2. Mary Jean Bowman, "Poverty in an Affluent Society," in *Contemporary Economic Issues,* rev. ed., Neil W. Chamberlain, ed. (Homewood, Ill.: Richard D. Irwin, 1973), p. 62.

3. Lee Bawden, quoted in the *New York Times,* May 12, 1974.

4. Rainwater, *What Money Buys,* p. 177.

5. William Simon, quoted in *The New York Times,* August 13, 1975.

6. Joseph A. Pechman and Benjamin A. Okner, *Who Bears the Tax Burden?* (Washington, D.C.: Brookings Institution, 1974). Only families at the very top and bottom of the income scale pay an average of more than 25 percent of their income.

7. Joseph Pechman, "International Trends in the Distribution of Tax Burdens: Implications for Tax Policy," an address before the Institute for Fiscal Studies in London, Oct. 30, 1973, reprinted by the Brookings Institution, General Series Reprint 284 (1974): 5.

Notes

8. Quoted in the *New York Times,* April 30, 1974.

9. Daniel Bell, *The Coming of Post-Industrial Society* (New York: Basic Books, 1973), p. 450.

10. Quoted by Mark R. Arnold in "The Good War That Might Have Been," *New York Times Magazine,* Sept. 29, 1974, p. 61.

11. Michel Chevalier, *Society, Manners, and Politics in the United States,* ed. John William Ward (Ithaca, N.Y.: Cornell University Press, 1961), p. 393.

12. Roger Wilkins, in *The New York Times,* July 29, 1975.

13. Arnold Cantor, "The Widening Gap in Incomes," AFL-CIO *American Federationist,* March 1975, p. 14.

14. Michael Manley, *New York Times,* Sept. 5, 1974.

15. Harvey Brooks, "The Technology of Zero Growth," in *Daedalus,* Fall 1973, (Issue on "The No-Growth Society"), p. 146.

16. Bertrand de Jouvenel, *The Ethics of Redistribution,* quoted in Irving Kristol, "Taxes, Poverty, and Equality," *The Public Interest,* 37 (Fall 1974): 28.

Chapter 12

1. Andrew Carnegie, *The Gospel of Wealth,* ed. Edward C. Kirkland (Cambridge, Mass.: Harvard University Press, 1962), p. 109.

2. John Dos Passos, *The Fourteenth Chronicle: Letters and Diaries of John Dos Passos,* ed. Townsend Ludington (Boston: Gambit, 1973), p. 281. (In a letter of 1920.)

3. R. H. Tawney, *The Acquisitive Society* (New York: Harcourt, Brace and World, 1920), pp. 4–5.

4. Robert Nisbet, *Social Change and History* (New York: Oxford University Press, 1969) p. 280.

5. Alexis de Tocqueville, *Democracy in America,* ed. Phillips Bradley (New York: Random House, 1945), vol. 1, p. 64. Italics added.

6. James Bryce, *The American Commonwealth* (New York: Macmillan, 1891), vol. 1, p. 538.

7. Percival Goodman, "The Concept of Community and the Size for a City," in *Urban America: Goals and Problems,* materials compiled and prepared for the Subcommittee on Urban Affairs of the Joint Economic Committee of Congress (Washington, D.C.: Government Printing Office, 1967), p. 59.

8. Ibid, pp. 179, 299–300.

9. Norton Long, *The Unwalled City* (New York: Basic Books, 1972), p. 183.

10. Abram Chayes, "The Modern Corporation and the Rule of Law," and Kingman Brewster, Jr., "The Corporation and Economic Federalism," in E. S. Mason, ed., *The Modern Corporation* (Cambridge, Mass.: Harvard University Press, 1959), pp. 25–45 and 72–84.

11. Theodore Roszak, *Where the Wasteland Ends* (New York: Doubleday, 1972), p. 130.

12. E. F. Schumacher, *Small Is Beautiful* (London: Abacus, 1974), Ch. 5.

13. George Feaver, "Vine Deloria," *Encounter,* 44 (April 1975): 39.

14. Robert Heilbroner, "The Human Prospect," *New York Review,* Jan. 24, 1974, p. 34.

Chapter 13

1. Simon Ramo, "Technology and Resources for Business," in *A Look at Business in 1990: A Summary of the White House Conference on the Industrial World Ahead* (Washington, D.C.: Government Printing Office, 1972), pp. 140–48, at 141. Subsequent quotations from Ramo come from the same chapter, passim.

2. Thomas J. Watson, quoted in the *New York Times,* January 8, 1970.

3. Committee for Economic Development, *Social Responsibilities of Business Corporations,* (New York: 1971), p. 59. Italics added.

4. T. M. Murphy, quoted in *Wall Street Journal,* Letter to the Editor, August 18, 1975.

5. Eli Goldston, "New Prospects for American Business," *Daedalus* (Winter 1969): 86.

6. G. M. Frederickson, *The Inner Civil War* (New York: Harper & Row, 1965), p. 201. Frederickson also refers to a more respectful reexamination of the medieval church as an influence, a point of view which Comte had set forth eloquently: a *secular* version of the church, to be sure, with science replacing God.

7. Thorstein Veblen, *The Engineers and the Price System* (New York: Huebsch, 1921), p. 136.

8. James B. Gilbert, "Collectivism and Charles Steinmetz," *Business History Review,* 48 (Winter 1974): 520–40.

9. Herbert Simon, *The New Science of Management Decision* (New York: Harper & Row, 1960), especially p. 48.

10. John W. Finney, *New York Times,* November 24, 1974.

11. An excellent summary of these and other views is provided by George M. Frederickson, in *The Inner Civil War,* Part III.

Chapter 14

1. Werner Heisenberg, "The Great Tradition: End of an Epoch?," *Encounter,* 44 (March 1975): 53. Italics added.

2. *1970 Joint Economic Report,* Report of the Joint Economic Committee of Congress, 91st Congress, 2nd session, March 25 (Washington, D.C.: Government Printing Office, 1970), p. 37.

3. Committee for Economic Development, *Social Responsibilities of Business Corporations* (New York: 1971), p. 60.

4. Heisenberg, "Great Tradition," p. 58.

INDEX

185

Index

Business (*continued*)
91; Southern opposition to, 30; support for poverty programs, 104; weakened by decline in social values, 134–135; *see also* Corporation

Business leaders, 33–36; as populists, 29; assimilated, 35; diversification of, 36; increased sophistication of, 139; meeting social needs, 153; and new motivations, 172–174; and preference for incrementalism, 138–139; as self-made men, 34; WASP origins of, 33–34

Byrom, Fletcher L., 88

Cantor, Arnold, 117–118
Carnegie, Andrew, 138–139
Chayes, Abram, 144
Chevalier, Michel, on American egalitarianism, 67; on American materialism, 41; on American self-government, 52; on American transportation, 26; on competition in America, 68; on liberty in America, 54–55; on work ethic in America, 44

Cities, as target for alienated, 131; dependence on social obligations, 130–131; reliance on military order, 159

City manager movement, 59
Clark, J. M., 119
Class, absence of in America, 67
Class consciousness, in America, 71
Coercion, relation to equality, 124
Coercive authority, 7–8
Committee for Economic Develop-

ment, 163; on business-government partnership, 152; on need for government regulation, 165; on need for planning, 168; on profit incentive, 153

Community Action Programs, 144
Community corporations, 144
Compensation, for unequal endowments, 105
Competition, as engine of growth, 89; diluted, 171; organizational, 74, 118–119
Competitive principle, 69, 101; modified, 74; necessity of, 75
Compromise of 1877, 31
Concession, to preserve social values, 17, 138
Congressional budgeting, 108
Constitutional value, 7–8
Constitutional value, American, challenge to, 90–100; effect of egalitarian drive on, 124; summarized, 64–65
Consumption, adverse effects of preoccupation with, 87–89; as focal value, 45–50; as national objective, 49; effort involved in, 48–49; major challenge to, 88; private preferred to public, 116; relation to work, 49; women's influence on, 46–47
Contract, as barrier to social legislation, 57; voluntary, 53
Coolidge, Calvin, 33, 75
Cooperation, inducing, 96
Cooperative workshops, 45
Co-optation, role of, 17
Corporate change, 166–167; initiated by government, 165; recommended by business thrusters, 166

Index

Equality (*continued*)
  monetary, 123; relation to compensation, 68; *see also* Egalitarianism, Equal opportunity
Ethnic confrontation, worldwide, 131–132
Executive dissatisfaction, 85–86

Finn, David, 85–86
Finney, John W., 183
Focal value, 6–7
Focal value, American, 41–50; challenges to, 79–89; shift from investment to consumption, 46
Food-stamp program, 106, 107, 110
Football, as entry to upperclass, 34–35
Ford, Henry, 84
Franchise, extension of, 27, 52
Franklin, Benjamin, on thrift, 44
Frederickson, G. M., 183
Freedom, as fallacious, 96–97; through planning, 151
Friedman, Dick, 33
Frost, Robert, 4
Full employment, as objective, 102–103, 169; inflationary effect, 103, 119; union support of, 114

Galbraith, John Kenneth, 37, 119
George, Henry, 56
Gilbert, James B., 183
Goldston, Eli, 153
Gompers, Samuel, 115
Goodman, Percival, 143
Goodwin, Richard N., 4; on individualism, 91–94

Government, as employer, 169; as initiator of corporate change, 165; cooperation with business, 151, 152
Government contracting, 169
Government regulation, as incrementalism, 140; inadequacy of, 173; limits on, 56–58; spread of, 60–61
Great society, as objective, 98
"Great Society" program, 99
Group identity, retreat into, 135
Group leaders, 21
Group values, 10, 135
Growth, *see* Economic growth

Hacker, Andrew, 4
Hamilton, William, 48
Harding, Warren G., 59
Hauser, Philip, 95, 99
Heilbroner, Robert, 4, 146
Heisenberg, Werner, 165, 175–176
Hoffer, Eric, 94
Hofstadter, Richard, 62
Home rule, 143
Hoover, Herbert, on competition, 70
Howells, William Dean, 46
Hughes, Charles Evans, 35
Hughes, H. Stuart, 35

Implicit bargain, 11–14, 138
Income changes, 113
Income distribution, problems of, 169–170
Income tax, opposition to, 58, 72
Incomes policy, 170

Index

Marquand, John P., 48, 70, 134
Mason, Alpheus T., 65
Materialism, American, 41–44
Mather, Cotton, on vocationalism, 42
Matz, J. Edwin, 88
Medical care, 106
Melville, Herman, 161
Meritocracy, 73; popular approval of, 101
Merton, Robert, 137
Metallic Lathers Union, 114
Military, as thruster, 157–161; greater reliance on, 158–159; involvement in cities, 159; relations with business, 158, 160; role, 157; subordination to civil authority, 158; values, 160–161; weakness as thruster, 162
Military-industrial complex, 160
Military life, appeal of, 161
Miller, William, 34
Morley, Charles, 178
"Muddling through," 139
Murphy, T. M., 152, 153

National Alliance of Businessmen, 104
National Commission on Causes and Prevention of Crime, 131
National Commission on Civil Disorders, 131, 158–159
National corporation, 32
National Labor Union, 56
National leadership, 24–25
National market, 26–27, 32, 45, 46
Natural aristocracy, 43
Natural community, 143–145

New leadership in business, viii, 22
"New property," 105
Nisbet, Robert, 142
Nye, Russell, 69

Objective conditions, changes in, 166; in value formation, 18–19
Okner, Benjamin A., 181
Optimism, in America, 3–4
Organization man, 36; as individualist, 62
Organizational competition, 74, 118–119, 169
Organizational cooperation, 174
Organizational revolution, 58; effects of, 118

Palmer, R. R., 51
Particularism, 135
Payroll taxes, 112
Pechman, Joseph, 112
People as constituent authority, 51, 56
People's democracies, 124
Perkins, Dexter, 25
Perkins, George W., 37
Pessimism, in U.S., 4
Philosophical validation, 15
Planning, French model, 168; for freedom, 151; need for, 97, 167–168; opposition to, 152; participation by business in, 168
Plutocracy, 71–72
Polarization, in American society, 117

190

Index

Simon, William, 110
Simpson, Alan, 24, 42–43
Skill, fragmentation of, 56
Skinner, B. F., 96–97, 99, 153
Slavery, effect on South of, 30
Social audit, 140, 173
Social Darwinism, 69
Social engineering, 151
Social entrepreneurs, 173–174; as thrusters, 175
Social-industrial complex, 151
Social legislation, 56–58
Social minimum income, 113
Social obligations, contingent, 129; deriving from social values, 130; eroded by racial division, 131
Social values, as national identity, 8, 11; changes in, vii, 18–21; continuity of, 17; defined, 6–9; development of, 11–15; of techno-centralists, 155–156; relation to social proprieties, 130; *see also* American social values
Socialists, as thrusters, 156; lack of organized base, 157
Society, as a system, 150
South, values relative to North, 30–31
Space program, 98
Specialization, 84–85
Spencer, Herbert, 69
Steffens, Lincoln, on business-government relations, 37; on individualism, 90
Steinmetz, Charles, 154
Success, as threat to values, 93–94
Systems analysis, as threat to individualism, 92–93
Systems solutions, 150, 155
Sumner, William Graham, 70

Tate, Allen, 30
Tawney, R. H., 141
Tax bargaining, 112
Tax incidence, 112
Techno-centralism, history of support for, 154–155
Techno-centralists, as thrusters, 150–156, defined, 149–150; opposition to, 152, 156; weakness as thrusters, 162
Technology, reliance on for growth, 82, 83
Thrift, 44–45
Thrusters, defined, 19; dependence on others, 20; entrepreneurial, 27–29; in groups, 21; influence of, 20–21; inside, 22; military as, 157–161; potential of, 149–163; social entrepreneurs as, 175; socialists as, 156–157, techno-centralists as, 149–156
Tocqueville, Alexis de, on American egalitarianism, 67; on American materialism, 27–28; on American optimism, 3–4; on egalitarian movement, 124; on popular opinion in U.S., 54; on popular sovereignty, 143
Trusts, opposition to, 56
Two callings, doctrine of, 42–43

Unionization, as product of egalitarianism, 119
Unions, *see* Labor unions
United Automobile Workers, 170
Universities, 33
Urban bill of rights, 95

192

DATE DUE

DISPLAY
Emphasis
'82

GAYLORD   PRINTED IN U.S.A.

WITHDRAWN